How to Be a Great Reference, and Get a Great Reference

How to Be a Great Reference, and Get a Great Reference

Tiffany A. Riebel, MSW

How to Be a Great Reference, and Get a Great Reference
First Edition

ISBN 978-0-359-00443-0

Copyright © 2019 by Tiffany A. Riebel.

Girl Scouts Handbook reprinted from *1913 edition*,
published by Skyhorse Publishing, Inc.

 Pope Francis, Holy Catholic Church

The author of this book does not necessarily represent the opinions of any names, institutions, and material in this book, nor any particular person or place. This book is not intended as legal or counsel advisement.
Image iStock paid for commercial use, no attribution required.

Lulu Press
Morrisville, NC, USA
www.lulu.com
1844-212-0689
Purchase this book at discount through the above distributor, or it is available through most online retail bookstores.

Printed in the United States of America and worldwide.
U.S. trade-ready print book.

Library of Congress Control Number 2018909292

ISBN 978-0-359-00443-0

4

Contents

Dedication

For all those seeking employment.

Help someone today; speak for someone today.

Preface

Those applying to college, work, or to volunteer, are seeking others to serve as a reference or recommendation; a person to speak on their behalf.

According to the (BLS) Bureau of Labor Statistics, about 62 million people, or almost 25 percent of the population, 16 years and older volunteered in 2016. At the same time, almost 70% of high school graduates were enrolled in colleges or universities, and those not enrolled in college were even more likely to be working or looking for work. Finally, the overall employed and working population at this time was at approximately 60% and climbing, among adults in the nation.

For most every person seeking to work, volunteer, or be admitted into college, there is an application component of a verbal reference review or letter of recommendation. With a required two to three person reference request per applicant, there is an outstanding need, from those with whom we have been associated, to serve as a recommendation.

The BLS cites a longitudinal report on number of jobs held. In this report, the young baby boomers held an average of 11.7 jobs from ages 18 to 48. Think of how many jobs or applications you have completed. From part-time or seasonal work, early career to late career, we have completed many applications and lists of people to serve as references. We need to know a lot of people, and a lot of people are needed to speak on our behalf.

Whether we are applying to college, work, or volunteer; applications and recommendations are a necessary part of transition to adult life. Developing yourself and establishing a career is necessary for gaining the finances that provide food, clothing, shelter, and life activity. A career is necessary for finding meaning in your life, and contributing to society, and the betterment of our communities. Furthermore, education, employment, and volunteer work provides daily healthy activity. Such life activities are a necessary part of every healthy young adult and adult life.

In a 2014 speech given in Italy by Pope Francis, the Pope comments about the need for work. He says, "*Not giving a job is not simply a question of not having the means to life: no. We can eat every day, we can go to Caritas* [charities, church *pl.*], *we can go to an association, a club, we can go there and they will give us something to eat. But this is not the problem. The problem is not being able to bring bread to the table at home: this is a serious problem, this takes away our dignity. And the most serious problem is not hunger, even though the problem exists. The most serious problem is that of dignity. For this reason we must work and defend the dignity that work gives us.*"

Our goals in education, volunteering, and work, give us dignity as human beings who are capable of self-reliance, helping others, and gaining knowledge that can be applied to world problems. When we achieve success, we begin to self-actualize and become who we want to be, and who we were meant to be.

Our roles in life, and our contributions to working for the common good of all, are a duty and obligation of life. It is our duty to help one another. It is our duty to work and serve with integrity and good skill. Our jobs give meaning to our lives, allow us to give back to others, and they make use of the talents that God gave us.

How to Be a Great Reference, and Get a Great Reference
highlights important components of each role. You will read
about how an employer can help in the interview and
determination of candidates; the different types of references;
how to be a great reference; and the qualities of character needed
to get a great reference.

Any act of goodness, a stride to help another, is an act that can
never be taken away. If you have heard of 'pay it forward',
'smile it forward', or 'pray it forward'; you will understand this:
reference it forward. Such a simple act of good reference, will
produce greater success for a candidate for the rest of their lives.
We must stand in solidarity with all those who need our help.
This action of good reference, and care for another, is an act of
altruism; not expecting anything in return for what I will do for
you.

The 1913 *Girl Scouts Handbook* (W.J. Hoxie), says that 'one of
the worse diseases nowadays is that people don't seem to have
the energy to stick to what they have to do. Whatever you take
up, do it with all your might, and stick to it.'
According to the handbook, Sir Boyle Roche said,
'I am not like a bird, able to be in two places at
once (this is really an enviable state, and I hope
the bird appreciates the privilege).' Now,
'supposing you had a fancy to have a lot of money
(and it is not a thing to be sneezed at), there are
many ways you could get it, provided that your
head is screwed on the right way...But before any
new employment can be taken up, you must begin
by learning about it now, so pave the way. Lay
out your plans and begin collecting information.
You will not have any luck unless you try hard.
Heaven only helps those who help themselves.
Luck is like a street-car: the only way to get it is
to look out for every chance and seize it--run at it
and jump on-- don't sit down and wait for it to

pass. Opportunity is a street-car which has very few stopping-places. CHOOSE A CAREER. *Be prepared* [as the *Boy Scouts* say]. Be prepared for what is going to happen to you in the future. If you are in a situation where you are earning money, think what you are going to do when you finish that job. You ought to be learning some proper trade to take up; and save your pay in the meantime, to keep your going until you get employment in your new trade...'

It is imperative that we be concerned at the rise in young people who are not establishing a suitable existence. Whatever the cause, the future must change. We all need to work, and to fulfill our duties in this life. I urge you to be a part of the solution for all employable people. A job means a better life, now and in the future to come.

This book *How to Be a Great Reference, and Get a Great Reference* welcomes all those who are involved in the employment process, with an abundance of helpful information. You will find information on Types of References; How to Handshake; Qualities of Good References and Qualities of Good Candidates; Marketing and Professionalism; Interviewing; Tools of the Job; Résumé, Cover Letter and Curriculum Vitae; Effective Writing and Thank You notes. There are sections about Human Resources and the Employer; information on Disability, Education, Tax Incentives, Social Security; Coaching; Problems and Problem Solving; and Planning for the Future.

Make good use of this employment handbook, and share it with your friends and colleagues. There is helpful information for everyone. Good luck on your applications and endeavors; I wish you all the best in life. Help someone today; speak for someone today.

Oath to Good Workmanship

Bound by the duties,
in this new position for which I seek;
where good people have spoken
in my honor,
and of the Gifts which God bestowed;
I promise to serve to the
best of all my abilities.

I promise to work with integrity, honesty,
and ever-improving skill.

I promise to serve others who are in need, and
to work for the good of all.

I promise to represent the best of the
candidate and worker.

I promise to carry forward the rights
of the applicant and worker
to live with dignity.

<u>*Confidence Mantra*</u>

I have the skills and strength

to fulfill my duties in work

and in life.

Introduction

My biggest fear with applying to every new job, was who to ask for a reference. I feared someone would say no, or that I could not find the right person, or even any person to serve as my reference.

The workplace should be a setting in which you enjoy learning and cooperatively performing your duties. Furthermore, the outcome of your work should be as polished as the process you took to get there.

You should often thank and recognize your colleague and peers for their contributions, skills, and achievements. You should thank them whether or not they work below, above, or on the same level as you do. Nothing builds cooperation and a stable, ethical environment like an honest thanks and praise. Learn from each other and discover ways to work together to achieve better results. Always be civil in the workplace. Treat everyone the same, regardless of how you personally feel about them.

A good human resource person will advise you that the best atmosphere in the workplace is one of civility. Keep your conversations lighthearted and genuine, be sympathetic when needed, and offer stories on your personal life only minimally and when appropriate. Ask others about themselves and get to know those around you. People like to be known, so introduce yourself to those whom you do not know.

If you have doubts or questions about your work, seek the advice of a supervisor, as directed. If it is permitted to seek the assistance of a coworker, be aware that their knowledge may not be as correct as your supervisor would instruct.

Display the best values and ethics for yourself and your profession. Nothing hurts your future as do questionable motives and actions. Furthermore, do not talk badly about anyone, at any time. Maintain a professional stance at all times.

Finally, tell your colleagues and peers that you enjoyed your day or week working with them. Highlight specific accomplishments and good work. Leave your day and job in a positive manner, such that you could call on a colleague anytime to serve as a reference of recommendation for employment.

Thank God every day if you have a good job. Remember to appropriately represent yourself in your education and occupation. Share your talents, skills, and achievements, but do so honestly. Know the requirements of your profession and maintain competence in your work.

Benevolence means the quality of being well-meaning and kind. First, do no harm, is the rule that all functioning adults should know. If you are going to school, volunteering, working, or have any contact with others; first pledge to yourself that will be of good help, and do no harm.

It is very important to learn how to be silent. Being silent and sitting with your own thoughts, and the quiet of those around you, is very important. When you speak unnecessarily or just to fill the void, you often say inappropriate or controversial things. When you do speak; say what you mean and mean what you say.

Develop yourself to be a wholesome individual. Go to church, volunteer in your community, do not liter, wear your seat belt, hold the door for others, eat healthy and exercise, learn new things, and give attention to the least among you.

Vouch (vouCH)
Verb

I am able to vouch for him.

To be able, from
your knowledge or experience, to
say that something is true; or to
confirm that someone is who they
say they are, or that they are of
good character.

Attest (ə'test)
Verb

I can attest to his knowledge.

To be a witness to, to certify
formally; provide or serve as
clear evidence that something
is the case
or true as claimed.

Handshake Etiquette

✓ Look the person in the eyes and smile.

✓ Grip hand firmly, but not tightly.

✓ If your hands are dirty or sweaty, give them a quick wipe.

✓ Be aware that all people do not like to shake hands, so take a second to view the approach of the person you are meeting.

✓ If you are offering sympathy, shake with your dominant hand, while enfolding the other's hand with your remaining hand. This is called a doubled-handed handshake.

References

&

Recommendations

TIP # 1

It is very important for an employee
to be aware of their actions at all times.
Think about consequences before you act.

Types of References

Professional References

Co-workers/colleagues - Co-workers or colleagues are a common and good source of reference. Colleagues are the individuals with whom we spend the most time and have the most shared experience. It is important to always be pleasant and cooperative with your coworkers, and offer to assist them at work when you are done with your own tasks. You should be friendly with your colleagues, and always keep your conversations lighthearted.

Customers - Customers can serve as recommendations only in certain circumstances. There are situations in which customers are to be maintained as confidential, such as in health care. But there are other customers who can provide business recommendations or good performance reviews. A customer should only provide recommendation of their own volition, and not by persuasion or coercion.

Manager or Boss - A manager or boss will not likely be your first source of reference, unless they knew you well. If you were a higher level executive, or your company was small, then you may be on a first name basis with your boss. Choose this source of recommendation only if you are going to be, or were in, an upper-level management position, or you knew your boss very well.

Mentor - Some people have mentors by way of friendship, guidance, or acquaintance. Others have sought out mentors through career networking or professional organizations. Seeking out a mentor is always a good choice for professional development opportunities.

Professor - You may utilize a professor as reference when applying for a job in higher education, or when applying for an advanced education program. Professors may often write a letter of recommendation based on their classroom experience of you, as well as on your grades and achievements. Sometimes a professor can also serve as a reference for a scholarship or fellowship offering.

Supervisor - A supervisor is a good choice of reference if you are in a specialized field, wherein you had frequent meetings or contact with your supervisor. This might also be a choice for reference if you were in a volunteer capacity, where as such, your overseer was a supervisor. A supervisor may use a standard letter of recommendation form, broadly expressing recommendation. If you need a specialized reference for certain fields, you will want to discuss this with your supervisor.

Character or Personal References

Community Leaders - A community leader may be a person with whom you volunteered, a church group leader, or extracurricular activity leader. These people are a great choice of reference and may have the positive, helpful outlook that are great qualities for a reference.

Pastor or Minister - A pastor or minister may be a good choice of reference if you are seeking admission into a parochial institution or church-related leadership role. Your Pastor should be familiar with you, by way of your active involvement with the parish and congregation.

Peers or Friends - While peers or friends may be an accepted form of reference, they may not always be professional. Peers and friends may not have a good idea on what criteria or words to supply when providing reference.

Terms in a Good Recommendation

Responsible	Knowledgeable
Attentive	Ethical
Reliable	Involved
Courteous	Honest
Pleasant	Motivated
Respectful	Leader
Helpful	Concerned
Hard-working	Trustworthy
Integrity	Obedient
Competence	Just
Smart	Efficient
Insightful	Skilled
Thoughtful	Capable
Timely or Punctual	Qualified
Virtuous	Polished
Well-spoken	Decent

Exceptional	Prepared
Valuable	Trained
Intelligent	Inclusive
Analytic	Gracious
Detailed	Polite
Precise	Confident
Accountable	Faithful
Dedicated	Prudent
Genuine	Temperate
Motivated	Creative
Experienced	Determined
Accomplished	Studious
Talented	Concise
Proficient	Succinct
Artful	Accurate
Savvy	Prepared

Being a Good

Reference/Recommender

TIP # 2

Be willing to help another at any time.
Offer to help before being asked and give frequent
reminders that you are available to them.

Qualities of a Good Reference

Concerned - A concerned reference is someone who cares about you and wants you to get ahead. They may listen to your needs and provide feedback. They are non-judgmental, and they will willingly provide a recommendation for you. They are benevolent, and remember to first do no harm.

Controlled - A controlled reference is the type of person who plans how they will go about providing the reference, and how it will be perceived. They know what to say and what not to say, and they stay within the boundaries of a good reference.

Giving - A giving reference is a person who appreciates what others have done for them in getting hired or admitted. Such a person sees this as a nice opportunity to do something for another person, and wants to give back in what has been done for them.

Impassioned - An impassioned reference believes in you, and believes in the need for a good recommendation for success. They value a good character and are not afraid to use optimistic terms with great persuasion. They will find out what you want, and provide it for you.

Objective - An objective reference views this duty as a service of the asking person. Such a reference will look at the applicant's good qualities and see the potential in them for the position or candidacy. They will be clear cut and firm in their task, and get the job done.

Powerful - A power reference is one who is grateful for their leadership role and are aware of the power that they hold. This person will pleasantly agree to provide a recommendation and will be content with the outcome.

Unattached -The unattached reference is willing to put adequate effort into their recommendation, and they expect nothing back. To this reference, the request is a mission and duty that they are happy to fill with no obligation or guilt expected.

Don'ts	**Do's**
Do not think of the negative aspects of your candidate.	*Do think of your candidate's good qualities.*
Do not mention any private or objectionable stories about your candidate in reference.	*Do think of good qualities, and objective and positive attributes.*
Do not favor one candidate over another.	*Do be strict in your analysis of an individual's assets.*
Do not exploit the candidate if you think their request is unreasonable, or for any personal bias.	*Do treat your candidate with the confidentiality afforded to any professional contact.*
Do not act irritated, frustrated, or inconvenienced by your candidate.	*Do give more than enough attention and understanding, reassuring as often as they need that you are happy to help.*
Do not assume that you know what the candidate wants you to say.	*Do ask the candidate for a copy of their résumé and accomplishments.*
Do not tell the whole story of the candidate's life, nor rush to give a listing of odd dates or events.	*Do pace yourself on sharing accomplishments, and offer it at the most opportune time.*
Do not take weeks to answer a request for recommendation.	*Do respond within a few days to any request.*

Thoughts to consider in your reference

1. In what ways have I known this candidate?
   Personally?
   Professionally?
   In the community?

2. How do I view them?
   As a maturing adult?
   As a well-respected leader?

3. I can think of times that I was impressed with them...
   Write down some of these times.

4. I can think of times when we worked well together...
   Jot down some notes on these instances.

5. I can imagine them filling this future role in what ways?
   Close your eyes and visualize your candidate at work or study.

6. Do I feel any negativity that I can reframe or set aside to better help this candidate?
   What is the negative that I see?
   Why does this person seem negative to me?

7. How will I respond if the employer asks me about the candidate's weaknesses or failures?
   Consider in your mind, scenarios of how you would respond.
   Remember to breathe, stay calm, and smile.

8. How have I been in a similar situation as this work candidate?

> Empathy is very important.
> How have you felt at these times in your life?

9. What good can come from providing a good reference?

> Spend some time imaging good outcomes.
> When you imagine another happy and well, you also feel happy and well.

10. How can I be a leader and advocate for this candidate?

> In what ways does this person need help?
> How I am well suited to assist them?

11. Would it be better to provide this reference verbally or in writing?

> The easiest thing to do is to ask your candidate.
> If you are worried about saying the correct things, you might consider preparing a well-written statement.

12. What are my apprehensions regarding this recommendation?

> Am I reasonable to be concerned about giving this person a reference?
> What would alleviate my apprehension?

13. How will my reference help this candidate, and contribute to their life success and happiness?

> What does the candidate hope to gain?
> What will be the benefits for them?
> What can I do to help this person?

Responsibility to your Candidate

Your candidate has requested a reference or recommendation; your duty and obligation is to them for a quality good reference. They thought enough of you and your leadership, to request this reference, and they have put their future in your hands. Believe enough in them to give a good reference. Do not provide every, or any, negativity, suspicion, or possible insight to this candidate's weaknesses. You need only to best help this candidate in their future endeavors.

Your Responses

Before you speak with an employer about a candidate, take a few minutes to prepare what you would like to say. *Positive adjectives* should be the substance of your speech. "Delightful, hard-working, honest." If you are not sure of what to say, peruse some of the adjectives on the aforementioned pages, or make your own list. Think about the candidate and visualize them at different times and settings. Close your eyes and see them smile, gesture, move about the spaces. What good do you see in this person? When we respond in a Christ-like manner, we encourage the perpetuance of good action.

Ethics

An administrative ethics aficionado will offer that you should not bring someone's personal life into the workplace. If you know something negative about a person, it is not to be mentioned, and not to be used against them. You *should* be admitted to a school, or hired for a job, because of your skills and your personal character. But you *should not* get rejected because of gossip, perceived troubles, or past mistakes. A person's past cannot always be hidden, but their stronger character or knowledge, because of their experiences, should be developed.

Mentoring and Coaching

If you feel up for the task of seeing this candidate through to success, be an active part of their life. Talk to them about their plans for the future, and be empowering *not* condescending. This is an acceptable time to be upfront with them, if you have any doubts or concerns about their abilities. When you speak with the applicant candidly, you may find that they are a more special person than you had first thought. Once they are hired, continue to communicate your mentee and ask them how things are going. They may want to seek your wisdom now that the doors of communication have been opened. Be kind and sensitive in your speech all of the time.

Liability

Most employers have a liability release form included with their references page. However, there should not be an issue of liability if you have the best intentions in helping the candidate. Your phone call, email, or letter, to an employer on behalf of a work candidate should be an answer to the question, "Why should we *hire* him/her?" If a candidate asks you for a reference, they are trusting you to be dutiful to give them a good reference.

Resources

What have you observed about your candidate? Are they introverted and quiet, or extroverted and sociable? Many candidates only know a select few responsible adults from whom they can seek a reference. You may not only be one of the select few that they know, but they may need to seek a recommendation from you on more than one occasion. Consider this an act of service. This should be an easy chance to help another human being.

Final Answer

If you feel extremely strong about not helping this candidate, then be upfront with them. Maybe there is a misunderstanding between the two of you that can be quickly resolved. If you are absolutely certain that you will not, and never will help this person, then you must be honest with them. But hopefully there are very few of these situations in the world that are so bad. When you help someone, they and their loved ones will always remember what you did for them. Similarly, when you do not help someone, they and their family and friends will never forget it.

Gracious

Be thankful to your candidate for asking you for this important recommendation. Your self-esteem will be elevated by your efforts to help them. There is so much reciprocal good that comes from helping one another. Practice collaborative empowerment.

Reframing Your Perspective

Your **good** recommendation is requested of a candidate. If you have negative opinions of your candidate, consider the following.

A new subject of study called Positive Psychology examines the strengths that enable individuals and communities to thrive. Positive psychology is founded on the belief that people want to lead meaningful and fulfilling lives, and to cultivate what is best within themselves and others *(Positive Psychology Center, University of Pennsylvania)*. Dr. Martin Seligman, a founder of this new area of study, advocates for the development of character strengths and virtues.

Similarly, renowned psychologist, Dr. Aaron Beck, a cognitive psychologist, would suggest that you try to reframe a negative perspective, into a more positive view.

Reframing Examples

Negative	Positive
Hyperactive ⟶	Fast, Quick
Loud, Noisy ⟶	Good Oral Communication Skills, Presentation Skills
Obsessive ⟶	Detail-oriented, Analytic
Intrusive ⟶	People Skills, Down to earth, Communicator
Insubordinate ⟶	Leader, Advocate
Takes too long ⟶	Hard Worker, Dedicated

Neural Correlates

As published in the journal, (PNAS) Proceedings of the National Academy of Sciences in the United States of America, an exceptional neurological study was conducted of the brain, in effect of the following:

- admiration for virtue
- admiration for skill
- compassion for social/psychological pain
- compassion for physical pain

Neural Correlates of Admiration and Compassion (2009) was researched by Mary Helen Immordino-Yang, Andrea McColl, Hanna Damasio, and Antonio Damasio. In this experiment, participants were exposed to narratives based on true stories, designed to evoke admiration and compassion in the above four categories.

The study was validated with fMRI images of the brain when shown these stories of admiration and compassion. The findings confirm that people have improved brain health when witnessing good acts in others.

The stories presented to the study participants illustrate scenarios in which professionals acted with skill, virtue, compassion for social/psychological pain, and compassion for physical pain.

All people want services from professionals who exhibit the traits of skill, virtue, and compassion. Imagine yourself seeking services from your bank, your roofer, plumber, physician, psychiatrist, minister, and professor. If you were disappointed with their services given to you, you felt terrible. Likewise, when you were impressed with the services given to you, not only did you advance in your life, your brain health improved.

We all regard competence and genuine care for ourselves and others as highly important. It is highly important! We are paying for the services we request, and we expect to get high quality results.

Imagine times when you were pleased with services for which you paid money. Or, imagine times when your loved one's health was improved after care. You felt happier! You were mentally clearer. Your brain was healthier because you witnessed with admiration the good accomplishment before you. Admiration can be evoked by witnessing virtuous behavior aimed at reducing the suffering of others.

Such virtuosic behavior is what every person involved in the employment processes must adhere. Employers and their staff must exhibit virtuosic skill to lead the organization in fulfillment of their good mission and values. Professionals must adhere to ever-improving virtuosic skill in their area of expertise, in order to provide best quality care, in accordance with their practice standards. Finally, recommenders should exhibit virtuosic communication with the applicant, and the accepting institution.

If our reference providers fail the candidate's expectations, or fail to help them in their request, the candidate's brain health retracts.

Reference providers must communicate well with their candidates, and have helpful and positive exchanges with them. It is unclear what percentage weight a recommendation holds in the hiring decision, so do your best to help the candidate.

Begin by smiling at your candidate, and say, "sure, I can help you." You will both be off to better brain health. The compassion and skill you show toward your candidate will permanently reflect in both of you.

TIP # 3

Refrain from diagnosing or sharing diagnosis
in your recommendation of a candidate,
and in any professional environment.
Do not diagnose your colleagues;
their personal life is not your business.

Getting a Good

Recommendation

TIP # 4

Introduce yourself to someone new every day.
Make your number of good acquaintances
exceed the bad.

How to Get a Good Recommendation

This is the book section that our candidates have been awaiting. What good characteristics will help you to <u>get</u> a great reference?

In a 2016 report outlined in a *Washington Post* article, Making Caring Common, a project of the Harvard Graduate School of Education, advocates students having 'concern for others' even more so than being overachievers. In a response to the report, a speaker for Yale University shared the plan to add a question to admissions applications, asking candidates 'to reflect on contributions to their family, community and/or the public good.' The University of Virginia agreed in 'promoting, encouraging, and developing good citizenship, strong character, personal responsibility, [and] civic engagement in high school students.'

Applicants should still strive for high grades and achievement, but how you apply what you have learned, is what is most important. What are you doing to make the world a better place?

Qualities of a Good Candidate

Accurate - A person who strives for accuracy does such things as carefully process their work, review it before submission, and concentrate on their task. You may use a ruler or guide bar to focus on each line. Accuracy may entail learning standard short hand, and following rules and guidelines explicitly. If you need to take a break before checking your work, then do so; it may help you to refocus and identify new errors.

Action-oriented - A virtuous person puts forth good and significant effort into what they are trying to achieve. If you are working for a certain cause, or dedicated to your line of work, then put more than adequate time into your projects. An action-oriented person seeks to identify ways to improve, in themselves, and in that which they do. Have the initiative to pursue what you do, and do it with the vigor in which your undertaking is worthy.

Communicative - Learn to express your thoughts in a capacity that works for you. Not all people may be public speakers, but you may write well, or vice versa. If you take a stand on particular moral or ethical issues, make certain that you have thought through what you want to say, and that it is not offensive to anyone. The basics of a good communicator is to know others' names, and say "Hello, how are you today?" when meeting.

Grateful - A person who expresses thanks frequently is a person who appears serious and respectful. Offer thanks after most interactions and communications with another.

Genuine - An ingenuous person is easy to recognize. Your facial expression should match your inner concern. Some professional codes of conduct instruct a genuine disposition. Being a genuine person means that you honestly care about other people.

Humanitarian - As a humanitarian, you care about the world. You do not have to be on the front lines of battle in order to be a humanitarian. You can volunteer, donate, recycle, or contribute to the betterment of the world in whatever way is best for you.

Humble - Humility is a key virtue in human existence. Being a humble person means that you know life is difficult. You do not express strong opinions in public, and you are sensitive to others' struggles. Your intention is to do no harm to someone who is hurting, and you often put others before yourself. Humility is defined as a modest view of one's importance, and it is realizing that everything we have is of God.

Introspective - Socrates said, "To know thyself is the beginning of wisdom." It is very important that you understand your motives and mistakes, in order to make self-improvements. Take time every day to reflect on ways that you can improve yourself. Think about your tone, reactions, interactions, and habits. Develop an objective awareness of yourself. *Objective: removing your personal feelings, about a person or situation.*

Modest - There is no place for immodesty in the work place or in school or volunteer settings. You must always be neatly dresses and covered. Gentleman might wear undershirts, and women the appropriate slips and camisoles. Skirts should be at the knee or lower, and shorts should never be worn in respectable settings.

Obedient - Obedience is compliance with an order, request, law; or submission to another's authority. You must obey your superiors, with the rare exception that there is substantive reason not to. Society thrives on obedience to our parents, to the police, to laws and policies, to teachers and professors, and to our employers. It is important that you do your best to follow the instructions of your employers. Obedience, in human behavior, is a form of social etiquette in which a person yields to explicit instructions or orders from an authority figure.

Organized - You must not only say that you are organized, you must actually be very organized. If you spend your free time making labels and dividers, then you are on the right track. When your desk is organized, so too will your mind and efforts be organized.

Polite - Ask permission from your superior for anything you need to do. While you may think your age, education, or status may exempt you from asking permission for minor things; it is still in your best interest to ask permission. Superiors prefer to know what is going on, and to approve employee actions according to policy and procedure. Always ask permission before doing anything out of the ordinary.

Punctual - A candidate who arrives on time, arrives late. Be at least a minimum of 15 minutes early. Show that you care: arrive, and arrive early. Your breaks and meal times should be strictly adhered. If on the rare occasion you are going to be late, call and let your employer know the reason why.

Regulated - A regulated person can monitor and control their emotions. Such a person looks at the consequences of choices and actions, and thinks before proceeding. Consider the Aesop's fable "Tortoise and the Hare", with the popular adage, *Slow and Steady Wins the Race.* Think about the consequences of wrong actions and re-consider your future actions.

Respectful - Be very respectful all of the time. To any superior, or older person, use the prefix Mr., Ms., Mrs., unless otherwise directed. Hold the door for another, or park your vehicle in a less desirable space to allow openings for others. Remember the special days (i.e. Boss's Day, Secretary's Day) of your family, friends, and colleagues.

Rule Abiding - Often employees sign forms without reading them. It is very important that you thoroughly read all documents that you are signing. This acknowledges that you understand and will abide by the agreed consent. If *a policy or procedure* is important to know, you should be able to apply it to your daily work. Read and understand all required policies.

Studious - You should keep a notebook of important information. When you have free-time in your day, use that notebook to review anything you may need to study further. It is good to attend lectures and educational talks pertinent to your line of work. Some professions require a certain number of continuing education credits per licensure term; so get your license and keep it active. Even if you are not required to learn for the remainder of your career, you ought to incorporate study into your professional life.

Well-dressed - Dress for the job you want, and dress for the person you want to be. Be aware of how you look at all times and in all places. A less qualified candidate who always wears a suit and tie, may get the job above a more qualified candidate in casual clothing. Be well-dressed and iron-pressed.

Compensation

It is important that you research and discuss your career path with the appropriate counselor. While you may have interest or skill in certain fields of work, the economic expectancy of a particular field may not be sustainable for your future.

You should be aware of salary ranges for the career that you plan to pursue. While some instances of salary range are a good starting point for negotiations, many employers have strict criteria for what is considered *compensable* experience. Similarly, some jobs' pay rates are entirely non-negotiable, such as is the case with union-managed jobs in public teaching and state employment.

Many of you will work for an employer, and complete what is called a W-4 tax withholding form, and then receive a W-2 as a year-end earnings and tax statement. Such employees can be paid hourly, or salary paid per year or per term. Other common positions are fee-for-service or freelance workers who complete a 1099 tax form. Still other jobs are small business owners with their unique documents.

You should speak with an accountant or firm that specializes in year-end taxes regarding all of these mandatory tax compliance forms. Familiarize yourself with the tax process, it will help you to grow professionally.

Pay inquiry and negotiations must be well-timed and restrained. Perhaps you find it best to ask about compensation when initially speaking with the employer at application. Other times, candidates ask at the end of their interview about pay <u>and</u> benefits. Finally, most candidates will wait until the position is formally offered to ask about compensation.

Stipends are fixed sums of money paid for services, or to defray expenses, such as for a fellowship, internship, or apprenticeship.

Risks for the Worker

Probationary Period - Probationary Period is the
minimum period of employment of six months of continuous
work. However, if an employer is a small business employer, the
minimum period of employment may be twelve months.
Probation is usually defined in a company's employee handbook,
which is given to workers when they first begin a job.
The probationary period allows an employer to terminate an
employee who is not doing well at their job, or is otherwise
deemed not suitable for a particular position. This probationary
period is more of an assurance to the Human Resource or Hiring
Personnel than any kind of security otherwise. An employee
must perform <u>at best capacity</u> during this time of performance
appraisal. If given a 2-week improvement notice, this serves as
warning of improvement needed or termination is possible.

Tenure - In effort to improve the quality of education, teachers
are granted tenure, based on annual or semi-annual evaluation of
their teaching abilities in the first years of work, and also based
on results of student performance in standardized testing. Tenure
can be granted for teachers of grades K-12, and for teachers in
higher education. Historically, legal debates such as *Brown v.
Board of Education* and *Serrano v. Priest*, have made strides to
protect student rights to learn. Tenure in the higher education
workplace may be based on such criteria as: quality research,
prolific and reliable work, making an impact in education, being
published, and bringing in grant money
(Discover Magazine, 2011).

At-Will Employment - At-Will Employment is applicable in
some, but not all states of the nation. An employee is always
at-will to leave an employer, but additionally, some states have
taken cause that they will be a state of *employers-at-will*. As
such, any employer may dismiss a worker at their discretion,
unless being done so as an unlawful discrimination.

Employment Law - Employment law or labor laws govern the rights and duties between employers and employees. Employment laws are based on federal and state mandates and legislation, and small party contracts. American labor laws began attracting attention in the 19th century and early 20th century in struggles for better working conditions and adequate pay. There are *explicit* (meaning very clearly stated) and *implicit* (meaning indirect or implied) rules of conduct in the workplace. Some of these include discussing pay, or discussing extracurricular events, while on the work clock. A good employer should act with justice, and the good of the worker. However, there are many instances, where laws are applied, and an employee has no recourse. Employment laws do vary between states.

Work is Work

I first heard the phrase, "reinventing you career", while doing a short-term position in the Career Services Center at the distinguished Kennedy School of Government. A book on the shelf was titled *Working Identity* (Ibarra, 2003), and it was about reinventing yourself for success amidst a career change.

Please take the topic of your work identity seriously for improving your professional self. If you are at a turning point in your career path, or feel like your career is at a dead-end; it is crucial that you define (or redefine) yourself as a professional.

Never settle for less than you dream and aspire. Work is work: it can be boring, tiring, disheartening, and overwhelming. But you must aspire to do great things with your life, and contribute to our world. If you do any work, you are a contributor to our world.

I expect that every able-bodied soul will seek their true path, and live an efficacious life of contribution. Whatever God's plan for your life; you serve a good purpose, so find your purpose!

Some career service centers such as the one I experienced have elaborate and helpful outlets for job seekers. With the new trends in career coaching, you might find a great career counselor with whom to speak, in your student services office. You may even find in your career services office, databases in which to search job openings, résumé review services, and individual rooms for phone interviews or video conferencing.

What you put into your work, is what you will get out of it. Every effort made to do something better, or help someone more, is an over-achievement that makes you better than the rest.

Every job comes with a degree of social responsibility. Social responsibility is an ethical framework for individuals and companies to act in the best interests of their environments and for society as a whole. Social responsibility, as it applies to business, is known as corporate social responsibility (CSR).

Labor Markets

Perhaps you and your parents or friends have thought about popular career fields in today's culture. You may see needs in your community, such as a person who is struggling, and it inspires in you a sense of need to help others.

I encourage you to pursue a career path that helps to make our world a better place. If there is a need in society, then there is a work vocation for you.

While it may sound cool to be a scientist or astronaut, ask yourself if this is the best path for **you**. Is it the best path for you? Is it a need in our society? Is it a job market that will allow you to flourish and succeed? Be the best of what you want to be.

Investopedia explains, "The labor market, or the job market, refers to the supply and demand for labor or work in which the employees provide the supply and employers the demand. It is a major component of any economy and is intricately tied in with markets for capital, goods and services."

The Brookings Institution is a nonprofit public policy organization based in Washington, DC. Their purpose is to conduct specific research that leads to new ideas for solving problems facing society at the local, national, and global level. (BIP) Brookings Institution Press offers books, library resources, catalogues, and an annual report on important findings that effect our society.

When you are searching for labor market data on potential numbers of job vacancies, salary expectations, and region locations for work, consider your sources carefully. *Credible sites* for labor market data will be those where the fundamental research and information is credibly obtained and verified for accuracy. Many of these such sites are institution-managed and based on real-time data.

While looking at data in labor markets, compare factual information and ratios for your career of interest. The (BLS) Bureau of Labor Statistics recommends these books:

1. ***Occupational Outlook Handbook*** is a biannually updated guide that profiles hundreds of occupations in detail.

2. ***Career Guide to Industries***, is a companion to the *Occupational Outlook Handbook*. It discusses more than 40 careers from an industrywide perspective.

Other sources for labor market predictions may include:
- State Department Agencies
- Research Organizations
- Professional Associations
- Online newspapers and magazines

TIP # 5

Take a course in record keeping.
Record keeping is valuable to know for yourself,
and in every business task.

Employers

TIP # 6

Evaluations of employees should represent
honest, accurate, and objective interpretation of
the employees' adherence to the
ethics and professional standards of
practice in their field.

Role of the Employer

The employer has the important role of taking in the most deserving, qualified and skilled candidate.

Getting to know your candidate

Confirm your candidate's education, credentials and work history. There are candidates who will embellish, or even lie, about their education and work history. It is important that you have a clear understanding of who you want to hire and why you want to hire a certain set of assets. Some roles for hire can be broadly defined, while others benefit from the specific criteria of certification.

You may find that the more important the position, and the more responsibility and decision-making authority the role will hold, that the more specific the candidate credentials and training should be.

Academic degrees can be confirmed through diplomas, or the candidate can request transcripts from their school for a small fee. State certifications and licenses can be confirmed online at the state department website. Work history can be verified for position and length of employment with respective human resources offices.

Learning about character and personality

It is very important that the employer truly see the person in front of them. Look into their eyes, and see the humanity and life experiences that they offer. Listen with insight into their honesty, and forthrightness of answers.

Does this candidate care about others? Do they understand dedication to their work? Does this candidate view justice and integrity correctly? Why does this candidate want this position? Do you get a good sense about their personal character?

Those most real answers about your candidate, you will obtain from sitting with them and studying them. Consider their dress, demeanor, gestures, facial expression, contemplation of responses, emotion, sympathy, knowledge.

Also, look at this candidate for discrepancies. If they describe being at a position longer than they have been an adult, or they say they are an expert on a topic for which they did not have education, then be wary.

Finally, it is necessary to do a background check. The most accurate and up-to-date information on criminal background will be found in these computerized record checks. If no record exists, but something still seems odd, you should both look at and listen to this person. If you feel significant concern for your safety with them, then you do not have to hire them, regardless of their qualifications.

Interpretation

It is very important to always use your objective analytical skills to interpret workplace problems and social situations. This means to think about people in the context of their life, their character, and their behavior in the social environment. Be cautious and honest not to misinterpret actions. To determine the root cause of actions, ask 'Why?' five times.

In resolution, you may consider problems from a policy, ethics, merit, psychological, competitive, sympathetic, faith, advocacy, seniority, legal, or economic perspective. Perhaps more than one of these, but your decision should be one that is the most honest, fair, and just. An employer has the duty to procure honorable work, product/services, and environment in their company. A correctly formed conscience will help you to know the right action with your staff. Your company will profit from doing the right thing, and it will reflect in the high quality performance, and in your satisfied and well staff and consumers.

Corporate Hierarchy

The organizational structure of a company delineates the ranks, responsibility and function among stakeholders, management and employees. The most commonly utilized corporate structure is hierarchical.

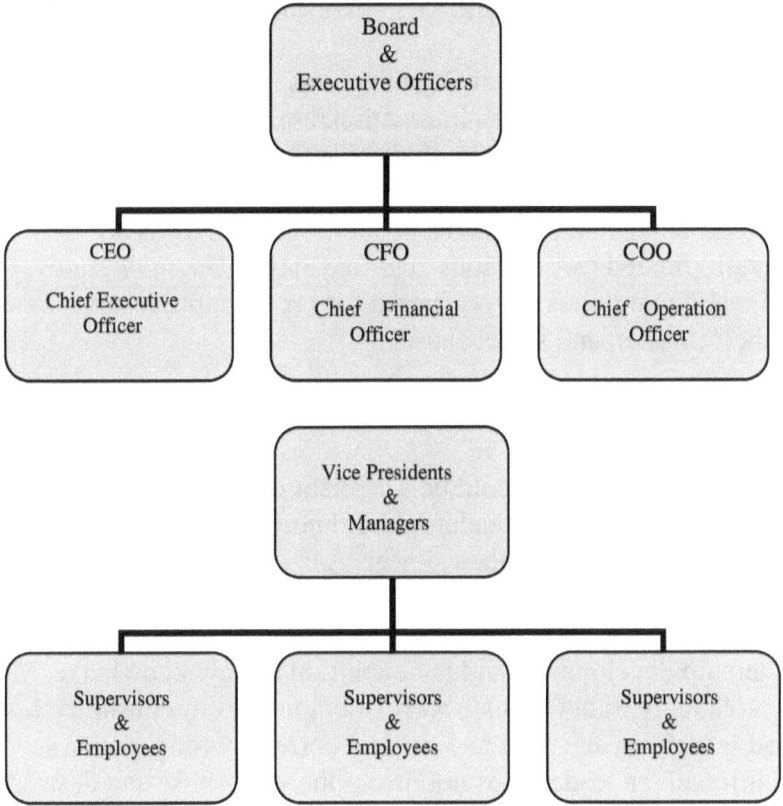

Structure options include: Traditional Hierarchy, Flattened Structure, Flat Structure, Flatarchy, and Holacracy. The more flat the structure, the more responsibility and equality each person holds. A holacracy identifies specific duties and decision-making among its employees, and is more common among small to medium sized businesses.

Roles and duties are assigned so that an organization flows well. It is important to follow the chain of command in the workplace, with a few exceptions. Such exceptions may include when there is a threat or danger, and when it is a matter of life and death. When life is at risk, you can make an effort to notify the right people. Make certain that you are correct when you make such statements.

(NGO) Non-Governmental Organizations

(NGO) Non-Governmental Organizations are usually non-profit companies, and sometimes international organizations, independent of governments, that are active in humanitarian, educational, health care, public policy, social, human rights, environmental, and other areas of *social good*. NGOs are typically funded by donations, and may have *charitable* status designation, and thus are registered for tax exemption status based on their mission and social cause.

Leadership and Values

A company's leaders should be a vigilant reflection of the goodness they wish to represent. Leaders should not align with others for the purpose of perpetuating their power. A chosen or elected leader serves their term to the best of their ability, and knows that eventually others will follow. Such a good leader encourages new leadership development and the evolution of new knowledge. More so, a leader does not speak poorly of employees or consumers. A good leader can see truth and lie, and corrects wrong action. Additionally, a leader does not discipline with abuse and destruction, but rather promotes right behavior through example and considerate education and counsel. Finally, a leader does not seek an end to life, business, or creation, but instead, sustains existence through moral application. Be cautious that your workplace is one of growth and health, and not of toxicity.

The phrase *Culture of Life* refers to morals as it applies broadly in many categories of life matters: morals in matters of life/death at all stages of life, from conception to natural death; morals in sexual activity and relationships, morals in bioethics and medicine; morals in media and design; morals in ethnic and cultural bias; morals in harsh discipline, murder, and persecution; morals in good and evil.

If a leader makes a mistake, which happens to everyone, he/she is able to take responsibility, and tries hard to prevent further wrongs. Such a good leader makes peace with themselves, with God, and with the one who was wronged. Finally, a leader is not self-serving, but rather empowers those beneath them to reach their potential and to flourish. Such a good leader can admit their strengths and weaknesses and encourages the growth of others. Seek leaders who are able to achieve honest and moral outcomes.

Due Process and Due Diligence

Due process applies to both procedural and practical aspects, regarding fairness in the methods used to make decisions, or to investigate a situation. Due process in the workplace may be for such proceedings as administrative determinations involving benefits, or employee promotion/termination.

Due Diligence is regarding the level of judgement, care, prudence, determination, and activity that a person would responsibly be expected to comply. Due diligence in the workplace applies to taking care to be thorough, predictive, transparent and accommodating of workplace conditions and decisions.

Accreditation

Accreditation is the process in which certification of competency and adherence to regulations are achieved. Accreditation is a process of review that allows organizations to demonstrate their ability to meet regulatory requirements and standards established by a recognized accreditation organization for safety and efficacy. Accreditation applies to both domestic and foreign organizations, and educational institutions.
Efficacy: the ability to produce a desired, or intended result.

(EOE) Equal Opportunity Employer

The U.S. Equal Employment Opportunity Commission (EEOC) is
responsible for enforcing federal laws that make it illegal to
discriminate against a job applicant or an employee because of the
person's race, religion, sex, national origin, age, disability,
or genetic information.
(U.S. Equal Employment Opportunity Commission)

4 Ways to Earn Employee Respect

Be Genuine - Be a good reflection of the mission
and values of your organization. Be respectful and
sincere with all workers, and speak considerately
with them.

Develop leadership - Encourage employees to be
leaders for the good. Allow them to speak and to be
heard. There are hidden leaders among your staff,
who will blossom and contribute to your success.

Develop potential - Promote greater success among
workers by speaking with them about what they
want for their career. Many employees are working
below their level of ability, and desire to be more.

Motivate - Become inspirational speakers in your
staff meetings. Smile, and connect with your
employees. Motivate them to be the best people and
workers they can be. Be proud of your staff when
they do good deeds.

Human Resources

TIP # 7

Do not accept or solicit colleagues for negative information about one another. This opens the channels for interpersonal problems and maleficence.

Human Resource departments offer a plethora of information for your employment experience. Human resource personnel can speak with you about benefits, compensation, orientation, policy and procedures, performance evaluations, recognition, learning and development, competencies, mission and values, retirement, and personal health and wellness programs.

Communication between the company and employee is critical to helping employees value their strengths, and in expressing appreciation for staff accomplishments. Human resource officers identify gaps, explain employee programs in plain language, and motivate and inspire employees.

Human resource personnel can also identify special needs accommodation for disabled employees. Human resources should be a welcoming and helpful environment.

Problems in the Workplace

When employees are at odds, and problems seem difficult to overcome, it is important to open communication and empathy for one another.

NY Times Sunday business columnist, *The Workologist*, gives friendly workplace advice. He has suggested that workers who are having difficulties do role playing and reverse roles. This will help to illustrate how others feel in a particular situation.

To role play, seat the employees face to face, and allow them to talk and interact. When people are hurt, they tend to avoid and shut down; so the opportunity to role play will open conversation. Preface the role play that it should not be offensive or destructive, but rather insightful and clear.

In her 1917 book Social Diagnosis, Mary Richmond suggests we look not just at the mental health/'irregularities' of a person, but that of their environment. This is called human behavior in the social environment, or (PIE) person-in-environment.

It is important for the human resource staff to consider the psychological aspects of an individual person such as pride, fear, worry, competition, relationships, culture/religion, knowledge, and defense mechanisms. To identify a core problem, you must thoroughly analyze the situation from a cognitive-social-psychological perspective.

The investigation of human behavior in the workplace is a newer subject of study termed Organizational Behavior or Organizational Psychology. Study of workplace behavior can occur at three levels within an organization: the individual, groups of individuals, and the organization itself as a whole.

Scapegoat vs. Bully

A *scapegoat* is one who is the subject of irrational hostility and intimidation. A *bully* is one who treats others in a cruel, insulting, unfortunate way, or coerces others to do the same. The bully is convincing to others, and encourages the mistreatment and isolation of an individual. Bullying begins very simply by saying mean things about another, which can include gossiping; and cornering, either physically or emotionally. *Gaslighting* is a severe form of psychological manipulation aimed to cause self-doubt. Abuse is never okay, and must be stopped immediately.

Confidentiality

Regardless of what the employee trouble, human resources professionals attain to confidentiality. Certain matters must be investigated upon report, while other information remains secure. Information that will not be shared, is your personally identifying information such as date of birth and home address. While other information, such as a problem with a peer or superior at work, will be shared only to the extent that security requires action.

If you fear safety and security in public-view positions, inquire into *exemption from public disclosure* status, if available. Some professionals work with dangerous consumers, others have a history in an abusive relationship, still others fear external interference from any number of peers, or even the media. Consider what your privacy means to you.

Ethics

One issue of ethics that often goes overlooked in the workplace, is misuse of power. Such misuse of power, is displayed from a superior toward staff beneath them. Misuse of power can portray itself as undue intimidation, unfair treatment toward a particular person, exaggerated discipline or evaluations, exploitation, and improper relationships.

Another issue is that of informed consent. Informed consent means that private information or proceedings cannot be acted on, unless the employee provides approval, thus protecting the interests of the employee. Examples of informed consent, may include: giving out identifying information of the employee; withholding information from the signing or contract of employment documents; and abrupt changes in contract or job description after hire.

There can also be ethical issues in the reading and data collection of anonymous surveys. If your company asks for the completion of anonymous surveys from either employees or consumers, they are to remain anonymous. There should be no deciphering of who completed the survey, nor retaliation against those who completed it. I repeat, there should be no retaliation from requested surveys.

EAP

(EAP) Employee Assistance Programs are usually free and available by phone with a Master's level certified counselor.

These EAP counselors can provide short-term, problem-focused brief therapy, or refer you externally with insurance-contracted providers.

Such brief therapy may include problem identification, goal setting, empathic listening, and referral suggestions. The counselor may ask you to rate your distress on a scale, and identify people in your life in which you draw hope. They may further offer ideas on effective interpersonal communication.

EAP referrals to external providers likely have no relationship with the EAP referring company. The external provider has only agreed to offer a set amount of counseling sessions at no charge, with the hope that the employee will continue in treatment, utilizing insurance billing for the remainder of needed sessions.

HIPAA privacy laws do apply in EAP counseling, except in life-threatening situations.

Lean Six Sigma - Toyota manufacturing invented the now very popular business strategy training called *Lean Six Sigma*. Lean is a complex program of business analysis using statistical mathematics and graphing to illustrate areas of needed improvement, and the suggested process to achieve such improvement.

Figure a.) Cause/Effect or Ishikawa Diagram Human Resource personnel find cause/effect diagrams helpful when gathering information to present to management.

What is the Social Security Administration?

TIP # 8

Anonymity is a more specific form of confidentiality, meaning completely anonymous. If you see your doctor out in public, they may show no knowledge of you, for the sake of *anonymity* or confidentiality.

What is the Social Security Administration?

The Social Security Administration (SSA) is a department of the United States government. It is an independent federal agency that organizes and administers Social Security, a social insurance program that prepares you for retirement. Speak with your local SSA representative to understand more about all of its programs.

All U.S. citizens have a unique nine-digit Social Security number. It is critical that you keep your social security number confidential and secure.

You may have heard advertisements about protecting your identity or 'identity theft protection'. Such a concern is very real. Unfortunately, there are cases in which a Social Security number is given to another, either by accident or by theft.

Instances of *identity theft* may occur for financial profit, citizenship application, or other reasons. Such violators are subject to criminal prosecution under the law.

Instances of accidental misuse of a Social Security number could be due to a typing error, similar name entry, or misinterpretation of numbers. If discovered this can be corrected.

Social Security numbers may change due to name changes and marriage. You must contact your local Social Security Administration for these changes.

Locate the Social Security Administration office in your local city, or visit on the web at www.ssa.org

A survey was conducted of
215 random individuals, ages 20-60

Question asked:

What do you consider your greatest success?

- 63 responded career and finances

- 52 responded education and achievement

- 45 responded good health

- 27 responded their children and family

- 18 responded overcoming loss

- 10 responded good luck and winning

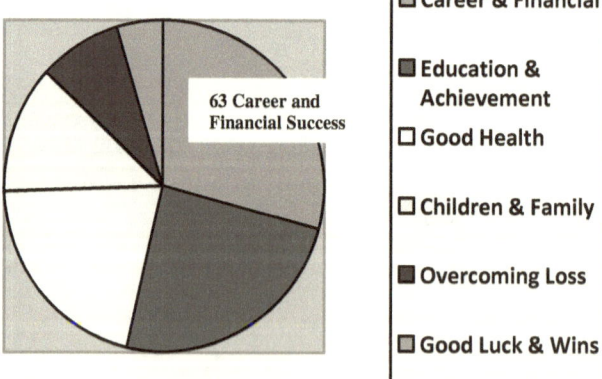

63 Career and
Financial Success

☐ Career & Financial

■ Education &
Achievement

☐ Good Health

☐ Children & Family

■ Overcoming Loss

☐ Good Luck & Wins

© Pates 2011

How to Interview

TIP # 9

Those who are shy or needing confidence, should perform *"as if"* they are confident, well-spoken professionals.

How to Interview

My college professor for Interviewing Skills was one of the best I had in college. Mr. Murphy taught us interviewing skills in an organized manner, and then provided a written test so to grade our mental understanding of the process. He then had us do real interviews, until performed entirely correct.

We sat knee-to-knee with our "client" to be interviewed, and went through the steps of the interview, one at a time, until performed correctly. He was not pushy or tear-invoking, he was nice and smiled as we tried our best. But we did it again and again, until we learned how to properly interview.

He would say, "now, let's say you are trying to interview a troubled teenager, and they say, '*you just don't understand; you don't get it.*'…then say to your teenager, '*teach me, tell me…*'"

The following terms are components of an interviewing.

Components of the Interview

Positioning and Posturing - Seat yourself in in front of your client to be interviewed. Maintain the distance appropriate for your setting. Dress respectfully and reservedly. Lean your upper body in, showing interest in what your candidate and employer has to say.

Greeting and Presentation - Smile, and extend a handshake if appropriate. Say, "*My name is…*" and await their name. Repeat back their name, to ensure that you heard it correctly. Follow with a '*nice to meet you*', or '*it's my honor to meet you.*'

Explanation - The employer can provide an explanation of the job opening and company mission. This will give your candidate a few minutes to calm down if they are anxious. Offer them a glass of water or a pen if need be. Speak slowly, and let them take in what you are saying.

Opening to the Client - Now pause and smile. Offer an upward hand motion to your interviewee, and encourage them to speak. Say to them, '*tell me about yourself, what brings you here...*' Interviewees should share briefly about themselves (education and experience), and how that relates to the job description and company mission. Candidates: speak slowly, and breathe.

Active Listening - Nod and smile while the interviewee begins to talk. Help them to relax and feel confident. Say things like, '*That's great*', '*Well done*', or '*I'm glad to hear that.*' Nod your head while the interviewee speaks to show that you are listening to them.

Questions - The employer can now begin with the questions and communication exchange with the interviewee. If you ask a question that your interviewee appears puzzled about, try to rephrase the wording of the question to clarify. Interviewee answers should be approximately 30 seconds in length, give or take, depending upon the person and depth of the question.

Open-Ended Questions - Open-ended questions are ones that provoke a more lengthy answer, and not a simple yes or no answer.

Closed-Ended Questions - Closed-ended questions do allow for a simple yes or no answer, or a choice of select answers.

Socratic Questions - Socratic questions are a philosophical style of critical thinking in which we are prompted to reflect on an answer. There are 6 types of Socratic questions: 1) Questions for clarification, 2) Questions that probe assumptions, 3) Questions of reason and evidence, 4) Questions about viewpoints and perspectives, 5) Questions that probe implications and consequences, and 6) Questions about the question. Socratic questioning of length is not a typical part of a work interview. (*Center for Critical Thinking*)

Suggestive Questioning - Suggestive questioning is when you infer or solicit the answer to the question, because you believe you already know the answer. Suggestive questioning is usually considered bad technique in objective interviewing.

Reflective Listening - Reflective listening is when you respond back to your interviewee re-stating their comment or idea. Reflective listening involves two key steps: seeking to understand a speaker's idea, then offering the idea back to the speaker, to confirm that the idea has been understood correctly. Reflective listening should not put the interviewee on the defensive, thinking they have said something wrong, but rather, it is to clarify that the interviewer has heard correctly. Practice reflective interviewing throughout the interview, especially when important points have been stated.

Summarizing - Both interviewers and interviewees can utilize summarizing skills. An interviewer will summarize once or twice during the interview to clarify and organize what has been said so far. An interviewee can summarize near the end of their interview, as scripted below.

Asking for Feedback - The interviewer will ask the candidate or interviewee for feedback and any questions. This is a good time for the candidate to show their good listening skills. The candidate can say, '*I understand that you are seeking a hard-working, responsible team member for your company. I know that the organization's mission is to provide good service...*'

Concluding - Both parties should offer thanks for the time to speak together, and the honor and pleasure of meeting.

Anticipating the Future - The employer may offer an expected time-frame in making the hiring decision. This is a fine time to ask the employer for their business card should there be any additional questions. Having their business card will provide the candidate the correct office address at which to mail the Thank You card as well.

You may now offer a closing handshake, and allow the employer to walk you to the door to exit.

Robert's Rules of Order

Henry Martyn Robert (1837-1923) was an engineering officer in the Army. From time to time, due to his military duties, he was transferred to various parts of the United States, where he found parliamentary chaos, since each member from a different part of the country had differing ideas of correct procedure. To bring order out of chaos, he decided to write *Robert's Rules of Order*. Robert's Rules is a standard providing common rules of parliamentary procedure for deliberation and debate in any meeting. This standard order is to place the whole membership on the same footing and speaking the same language. Roberts Rules provides for constructive and democratic meetings, to help, not hinder, the business of the meeting/assembly. You will find most <u>club meetings</u> today organized under a shorter variation of the following, typically called <u>meeting minutes</u>.

- Point of Privilege
- Parliamentary Inquiry
- Point of Information
- Orders of the Day (Agenda)
- Point of Order
- Main Motion
- Divide the Question
- Consider by Paragraph
- Amend
- Withdraw/Modify Motion
- Commit/Refer/ Recommit to Committee

- Extend Debate
- Limit Debate
- Postpone to a Certain Time
- Object to Consideration
- Lay on the Table
- Take from the Table
- Reconsider
- Postpone Indefinitely
- Close Debate
- Committee of the Whole
- Appeal Decision of the Chair
- Suspend the Rules

Building a Résumé
or
Curriculum Vitae

TIP # 10

Have several different people review
your résumé. Each may have different
and helpful feedback.

Sample Résumé [First M. Last Name]
City, State
Phone-Email

Objective
Seeking to utilize my skills in a team-oriented position, in communications and marketing.

Education
Bachelor of Arts, English   GPA 3.8
University of New England
City, State

Certified Publisher   2015
Expert Stats

Professional Experience
Team Lead   Dates-Dates
Caritas Services   City, State
-Designed marketing framework on large-scale
-Created user-friendly database to maximize

Intern   Dates-Dates
Cloud One   City, State
-Led team meetings and presented work
-Maintained 95% perfect ratings in online site

Volunteer
Team Captain   2012-2014
Special Olympics Sports

Awards
Perfect Attendance   2010
Dean's List Honor Roll   2012, 2013, 2014

Publications
Young Adults Take the Lead
Business News in Town   April, 21, 2016
It's the Details that Matter
Company Bulletin   June 13, 2016

Special Skills
- Web Design
- Spanish-speaking, proficient

Sample Cover Letter

Name
Address
Phone number
E-Mail Address

<5 spaces>

Month Day, Year
<2 spaces>

Dear Mr./Ms.[Name] **or** Respected Managers at [Company]:

I am writing in application to the advertised position of [title] number [position listing ID] with [Company]. I am eager to express interest with your company and this position because [state your reasons].

I offer strong assets to this [title] position with [Company], including [list some of your outstanding qualities]. My education is in the [specify] field, with a degree(s) in [fill in your degrees], from the university/college of [college name].

My professional experiences have afforded me great opportunity to learn about [what have you learned?]. These experiences will make me a valuable member of your work team, and the customers you serve.

In my past positions, I was able to [site specific accomplishments, such as sales, results, and percentages].

I have heard and read great things about [Company], and look forward to meeting to further discuss this opportunity. [Further elaborate on something positive you know about the company, such as mission and values].

<3 spaces>

Sincerely,
<2 spaces>

[ink sign your name]
[typed name]

Curriculum Vitae
[the] course of [my] life

A curriculum vitae is a written summary of educational and professional experience. It is more commonly used in teaching, research, and advance degree settings.

Difference between a résumé and a curriculum vitae

Résumés are brief, and preferred to be only about one page in length.	A curriculum vitae is more detailed, and may be up to several pages in length.
Résumés list only essential information.	A curriculum vitae will be a complete and detailed listing of all work and related activities.
Résumés have a typical format, simple font, and are center justified.	A curriculum vitae is open to personal styling, but is always reserved and professional.
Résumés are an easy format for any application or submission.	A curriculum vitae is used by researchers and professors, with published works and recognitions.
Résumés are a quick compilation of all of your accomplishments.	A curriculum vitae may include descriptive paragraphs on specific work.

While a (CV) curriculum vitae is left to personal styling, it should still be uniformly developed throughout. Headings, margins, and section dividers should be constant throughout the document. A CV is left justified on the page, as it will contain more written content, rather than just bullet points as in a résumé. A CV should appear highly professional and polished.

Particular to one's occupation, there may be a section on the curriculum vitae about your measured achievements, such as: scientific data sets, book and journal sales ratings, performance standards in the arts, or even film production highlights.

There are interesting variations on the curriculum vitae between countries. A U.S. curriculum vitae remains objective with only professional data, while an European curriculum vitae may include marital status, number of children, age, secondary education, and personal interests.

Your résumé or curriculum vitae listings should be in chronological order, with the most recent event first in each section. Always begin with education/degrees, followed by work experience, and then additional sections as needed.

Finally, all type in either a résumé or curriculum vitae, should be of a readable font, such as Times New Roman. Use **bolding** selectively, for section headings, school names, or degrees earned. Italics may be used for book, song, movie, and other published titles. You can find paper specifically for résumé/CV printing at college bookstores and office supply retailers.

Expanding on Your Work

Your résumé is a brief listing of job and work performances. But at some point in your application and interview process, you will need to be more specific about what makes you a special and unique candidate.

There is an acceptable time and place to be proud of your accomplishments. Be proud of your accomplishments in an application, be proud of your accomplishments on your professional profiles, and be proud of your accomplishments when going on an interview.

Regarding the job description for the position which you seek, you must consider the duties of the position in light of what you can/cannot do, and in what you like/dislike to do.

Job descriptions are not always complete or thorough enough for what the job will actually entail. So, use your imagination to elaborate on what duties with which you might be faced, and consider if it is a good fit of job for you.

When you do apply and interview, present yourself in unique and individualized ways in comparison with the job for which you are applying. Tell the employer, *"I am a good candidate because...."* Choose your words carefully, but be proud. Stand out from the crowd and let yourself be the shining star that you are.

Requesting a Professor/Faculty Recommendation

Requesting an important professor or faculty recommendation is acceptable for such things as internships, graduate school in the field, fellowships/scholarly studies, and possibly study abroad.

It is impossible for professors to recommend every student that they taught, so plan early if you anticipate needing the help of a professor.

Good ways to be a standout student to your professors are to participate in class discussions, volunteer to help when asked, meet with the professor during scheduled office hours, and become involved in and out of the classroom.

A well-written letter from your most admired professor, who is sure to remember you, means more than a generic letter from the dean of the school. Put emphasis on your skills and concern for the field of work that you intend to pursue.

Know in advance when you will need the professor's letter of recommendation, and arrange a time to speak with them at least a month in advance.

If you feel very strongly about the endeavor which you are about to pursue, then be upfront with your professor about needing a strong recommendation. State your accomplishments, coursework completed, and your plan for your future, with the professor.

If you reach out to your professor's secretary or assistant first, succinctly state the reasons why you need to speak with the professor. Then suggest that your student file or transcript be requested prior to seeing the professor.

When you meet with the professor, present yourself well in appearance and professionalism. Bring with you a copy of your résumé or curriculum vitae, along with the specifics of the needed recommendation, such as length requirements and deadline.

Verbs in a Good Résumé

Each descriptive bullet point or paragraph in your résumé or CV, should begin with a descriptive verb. Choose the best verbs for the great work that you are explaining. These verbs will almost always be written in the past tense.

Administered	*Illustrated*
Adapted	*Influenced*
Analyzed	*Increased*
Applied	*Initiated*
Assessed	*Investigated*
Assembled	*Led*
Brainstormed	*Logged*
Briefed	*Managed*
Built	*Monitored*
Calculated	*Publicized*
Conducted	*Programmed*
Coordinated	*Satisfied*
Created	*Scheduled*
Designed	*Secured*
Determined	*Supervised*
Developed	*Strategized*
Diagnosed	*Strengthened*
Directed	*Surveyed*
Distributed	*Summarized*
Drafted	*Synthesized*
Edited	*Taught*
Empowered	*Tracked*
Ensured	*Transformed*
Established	*Updated*
Examined	*Verified*
Expedited	*Welcomed*
Highlighted	*Wrote*

Marketing Yourself

&

Professionalism

TIP # 11

Enhance your vocabulary by reading and
writing. Always keep a dictionary and
thesaurus on your desk
for quick reference.

Self-Development

What are your character strengths?
- ✓ Bravery
- ✓ Creativity
- ✓ Fairness
- ✓ Humor
- ✓ Judgement
- ✓ Kindness
- ✓ Excellence

What are your character virtues?
- ✓ Patience
- ✓ Gentleness
- ✓ Humility
- ✓ Fortitude
- ✓ Faith
- ✓ Temperance
- ✓ Justice

What do I enjoy doing?
- ✓ Learning
- ✓ Music
- ✓ Dance
- ✓ Reading
- ✓ Theater
- ✓ Travel
- ✓ Church

What could I study more about?
- ✓ Culture
- ✓ Nature
- ✓ Arts
- ✓ Religion
- ✓ Classical Music
- ✓ Volunteering
- ✓ Writing
- ✓ Health

Presentation

Pieces of a Suit

A suit, which is derived from the French word "suite", because of matching the pants to jacket, is worn as a sign of respect.

The parts of a suit coat are typically the same for men and women, consisting of collars, lapels, gorges, pockets, vents, pleats and cuffs. However, the cut or silhouette, of a man's jacket is different from that of a woman's jacket. Men's jackets are boxy in shape with only minor detailing through the midriff, whereas a woman's jacket will be more fitted, possibly with more seaming, and smaller lapels. In men's pants there are generally two types, pleated and flat front. Women have the additional option of choosing either a pant or skirt.

Specialty design elements of the suit for men may include silk interior and pockets, as well as quality buttons and a boutonniére slit. For women, additions may be in the form of silks, cording, lace and extra buttons.

The color palette for a man's suit is generally reserved to black, navy, brown, charcoal, tan or deep olive. There are simple woven patterns such as thin pinstripe, herringbone, tweed, or a muted plaid for the jacket. Women's suits allow a broader ranges of hues, and solid color choices, depending on seasonal favorites. Patterned fabric may include plaid, tweeds, herringbone, and stripes. The weight or thickness of the suit fabric should be selected accordingly to season and temperature. For example, wool suits are more appropriate for the cold seasons, while linen or crepe fabrics are more appropriate for the warmer months.

Men wear shirts and usually matching ties under their suit jacket. A woman may wear a blouse or any appropriate, but not revealing garment.

Many suits are dry clean only, but there are select retailers which sell machine washable suiting. Similarly, suit fabrics may not allow for ironing, but be okay to steam press. Always read the labels to ensure proper care for your professional attire.

A suit should be worn to most interviews of a professional nature. While you can choose your clothing as best suits your personality and work environment, you should always be polished and reserved. Additionally, limit your makeup and perfumes on the job.

Email, Cell Phones, and Social Media

Email can be a quick, convenient and very efficient method of communication when used correctly. Email should only be sent to those who wish to receive it. Furthermore, if your email is to be used in a professional setting, it may need to include a confidentiality disclosure.

Email should be respectful and well-written. It is preferred they not be lengthy, but get directly to the point. Emails should begin with Dear Mr. / Ms. (respectively), or Good Morning / Good Afternoon. You should succinctly explain the *Who, What, When, Where, and Why* of what you are relaying. Finally, always close your emails with a sincere thanks, your name, and your position title.

Cell phones are banned from most professional settings. Cell phones can be a distraction, inappropriate use of work time, and a breach of confidentiality in the workplace. Some settings allow cell phone use only on phones that the company provides, as they are necessary to complete tasks. Other professionals who are independently employed may use a cell phone to conduct their business. Cell phones were created for the purpose of safety and connect-ability; but they are not an extension of your person.

Social media profiles that allow for professional networking are permissible in most cases. However, any inappropriate, vulgar, or explicit content on social media sites, will be found, and will negatively impact your life. Furthermore, do not have multiple, incomplete, abandoned profiles on the web; clean up your internet profiles, and maintain their accuracy. Never talk about intimate details on the internet; remain professional at all times.

Effective Writing

One of the most useful classes that I took in high school was journalism. It taught me how to interview, communicate, find important highlight information, and to be organized, accurate, and succinct in my writing.

English class with a good instructor is very helpful in learning how to write well and structure a quality paragraph. The first sentence of a paragraph should give insight into what the paragraph will be about. Then provide two to three sentences that give proof or example in support of the paragraph topic. Finally, you will have a closing sentence that briefly summarizes the paragraph points or topic.

It can be helpful to create an outline of your paragraphs on index cards prior to putting them on paper. A completed paper will have at least one opening and closing paragraph, to present and then conclude the purpose of the paper.

Effective Writing Checklist

- ➢ Writing has a clearly defined purpose
- ➢ The information in your writing is clearly arranged and organized
- ➢ There are numerous supporting points that are identified, labeled, and transition smoothly throughout the paper
- ➢ Word choices are correct and advanced to your level of education
- ➢ Sentences are complete and portray appropriate tone and affect
- ➢ Remove all *conjunctions*: can't, won't, didn't, aren't; instead write both words out
- ➢ Your writing has been reviewed and edited several times, over a period of days to ensure error finding
- ➢ Research is adequately cited per your teacher's instructions

Thanks You Notes

&

Gifts

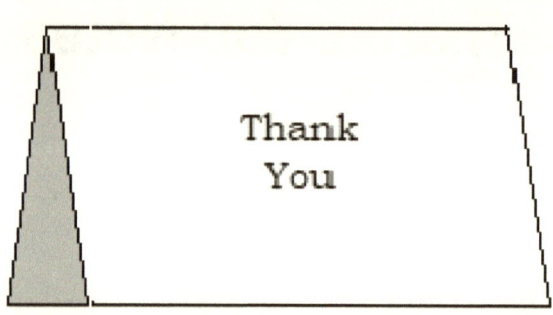

Thank
You

How to Write a Thank You Note

o   Choose a simple style, small note card

o   Make sure you are correctly spelling the
person's name

o   Begin with the two most important words,
"Thank you…"

o   Add detail about why you are thanking them

o   State your interest again in the specific position

o   Remind them of the great skills you would
bring to the job

o   Anticipate the future with a statement of
"hope to hear back"

o   Sign with a sincere thanks for their time and consideration

o   Review for spelling errors; if you need to start over with a new
card, do so, or always
practice on scratch paper first

Gift-Giving in the Workplace

Gift-giving in the workplace is kept to a minimum. Gifts are
generally not considered a good idea. There are a few rare
occasions that are acceptable, such as a holiday gift swap, or for a
special occasion such as Boss's Day. If you do give a gift, keep it
under a certain price, such as $15. If you agree to contribute to the
cost of a group gift, remember to turn in your portion of the
money.

It is <u>inappropriate</u> to bribe with gifts, or to make exchangeable offers.

TIP # 12

Spend time reflecting on your day.
Consider on a regular basis what you
could do to improve yourself.

Coaching

TIP # 13

Speak well of your customers and colleagues.
They are your professional life
and your personal success.

Pillars of Coaching

Coaching is a specialty practice, just like any other work specialization. A doctor may specialize in pediatrics, oncology, pathology, etc. A coach is trained in specific methodology as well and adheres to certification and training requirements. Just as a therapist is trained in psychology and therapeutic interventions, so is a coach trained in their work. Do not attempt to do anything for which you are not specifically qualified to do, as it will likely do more harm than good.

You may however, be an encouraging and compassionate person, with an organized presence in helping others. Be reserved in your approach when speaking with others, and always be nice. Believe what others share with you, and be sensitive to who they are, and to who they want to be.

You may consider the basics of these pillars of coaching when speaking with others.

Culture - Culture can refer to race, ethnicity, religion, cultural traditions and ways of thinking. Culture can also mean the culture of a group of individuals in today's society. For example, perhaps there is a phrase or media following that is known among people of a certain region. *Paradigm*, broadly defined, is a philosophical or theoretical framework of any type. Similarly, an *axiom* is an idea regarded as being accepted, or evidently true. *Meme* is an image, video, word, or phrase that is shared among a group.

Empathy - Feel for others' suffering and struggles. A leader is an action word, not a title. A leader goes forth with understanding, goodness, and wanting the best for others. They do not manipulate or demean for their own pride. Rather a person of empathy can see with insight into the real intentions of another, and wants to see to others' wellness and success.

Motivation - Encourage your client to reach their potential; help them to better recognize their strengths. People are motivated to repeat the experiences they know that have made them feel good. Thus, we need to cultivate more positive experiences. The brain regulates fear and threat, as well as happiness and optimism. You must be able to see ahead into the possibilities in the future. You can instruct that we all need to leave our comfort zone to grow and mature gracefully. Speak with charisma and be encouraging and hopeful.

Organization - It is important to keep your mind and work organized, and on task. This is not just for your mental health, but also for your professional and personal growth toward leading a calm and productive life. It is vital that you live your life in truth: on the truth of where you are, and where you want to be. An organized person remembers the important points of a conversation or topic for the purpose of use in the future. You should organize your mind and work, as well as your home and leisure activities.

Structure & Pedagogy - Develop a standard method of approach in each session and maintain this standard of approach throughout your coaching sessions. Just as a cognitive therapist will begin and end a therapy session with review, so too must a coach. A coach should teach with confidence, lest they offend their clients and show defensiveness in themselves. Knowledge and wisdom are not mutually exclusive terms: they intermingle with prudence; in knowing what you know, and knowing
if, when, and how to act.

Virtue & Integrity - A virtuous person puts forth their best effort for the best causes. A virtuous person recognizes the need for self-improvement and takes steps to work toward that improvement. Virtue can be patience, kindness, gentleness, modesty, self-control, wisdom, knowledge, fortitude, temperance, generosity, joy, charity, hope, faith, love, understanding, justice and peace. A person of integrity is a conscience-driven person who will correct their mistakes. They remain constant to doing what is right. By their own free will, the virtuous and integrous persons are honest and upright. Such a person is known to have a good character.

Certified and credentialed coaches are outstanding leaders. Many impressive coaches have achieved significant change for the betterment of our world. Carol Kauffmann PhD received a $2,000,000 award to create the Institute of Coaching at McLean Hospital/Harvard Medical School. She is a leadership coach with numerous publications and "prestigious efforts to help leaders raise the bar on their performance, and manage their success."

Coaching is a more recently popular, wide-spread field for entrepreneurs who may consult with large and small firms. Such consultation aims to provide feedback and reformation on organizational styles. But coaching is not solely for the business-minded.

Coaching is based on the theories of positive psychology, building others up based on their strengths, rather than creating resistance in their weaknesses. This applies to the healthy and unhealthy, rich and poor, men and women, all alike.

New York Times Bestseller, *Happier* (Ben-Shahar, 2007), says, "The right employer can create conditions that are conducive to happiness." Social and Organizational psychologist Richard Hackman explains certain conditions that can lead an employee to experience more meaning in their work. He lists the following:

1. The work should draw out a variety of talents and skills
2. The employee should complete the whole task, from beginning to end
3. The employee should feel that his/her work has a significant impact on others

On 'Finding Our Calling', Dr. Ben-Shahar writes, "Psychologist Abraham Maslow once wrote that 'the most beautiful fate, the most wonderful fortune that can happen to any human being, is to be paid for doing that which he passionately loves to do.'"

Similarly, Professor of Organizational Psychology at Yale, Amy Wrzesniewski, suggests that people experience their work in one of three ways: as a job, as a career, or as a calling. She says that people can find meaning in their work, and that will make workers more satisfied in their life. In a talk aired on *Coaching with Copeland*, Amy and colleagues from Wharton School of Business and other top schools, conducted long-term in-vivo research on motivational factors for work. One such study focused on 10 cohorts of West Point cadets for 14 years, using a sample of about 10,000 people. They found that strong internal motivations were a powerful and positive contributor. Also learned, were factors of the honor and prestige with which future employers might view them. Dr. Wrzesniewski says that we should never lose sight of the reason we are doing whatever we are doing; to do good and to find meaning.

Motivation

Depicted in a pyramid, Maslow's hierarchy of needs theory explains the different levels of human psychological and physical needs. This can be used by business managers to better understand employee motivation. The needs in Maslow's hierarchy include the basic physiological needs (food and clothing), safety needs (job security), social needs (friendship), self- esteem, and self-actualization (achievement of who you want to be).

Other psychologists on motivation:

- Clayton Alderfer's theory of ERG: Existence, Relatedness, and Growth
- David McClelland's Need Theory of three motivational paradigms: Achievement, Affiliation, and Power
- Frederick Herzberg's Two-Factor Theory of intrinsic and extrinsic motivators
- John Stacey Adams' Equity Theory in employee/organization relationships
- Victor Vroom's Expectancy Theory: expected results and desired results as motivators of behavior
- Shalley, Locke, & Latham's Goal Setting in Business
- Piers Steel & Cornelius J. König's (TMT) Temporal Motivational Theory

Problems

&

Problem Solving

Mental Health First-Aid
Mental Health First Aid Act of 2015
Senate bill 711
House of Representatives bill 1877

➤ Recognizing the symptoms of common mental illnesses and substance use disorders

➤ De-escalating crisis situations safely

➤ Initiating timely referral to mental health and substance abuse resources available in the community

Find a training online or near you today.

Identification of Problems

Inter-Office Relationships

Romantic relationships in the workplace are a big no-no. It is
not a good idea to date your co-workers, and it is never a good idea
to have a 'fling'. Dating a co-worker is awkward for the
two involved, and for colleagues witnessing it. There are a few
exceptions to this rule, such as if the two people are intending to be
married. Be cautious though, that couples in the workplace
can be a point of controversy, and is typically frowned upon.

Over-Disciplining

There are times when employees are over-disciplined. This can take
the form of an exaggerated evaluation, inconsistent grading, wrong
tallying, being cited more than once for the same mistake, and
carrying forward the guilt or error for a mistake into the
future. Just as parents provide direction to their children, so managers
provide direction to their staff. However, there is a difference
between providing direction, and abusing your staff. The purpose of
disciplining is to prevent, intervene, and instruct, so that the employee
is an even better employee in the future. If you are uncertain how to
evaluate, then wait, or proceed benignly.

Wearing Too Many Hats

It is almost always problem-causing to have dual-duties and dual
relationships in the workplace. For example, you should not be
supervisor, brother, and best friend. Serving multiple roles at work,
and having colleague friendships outside of work can create ethical
problems. It is best to remain in a distinct work role, and maintain
benevolent friendliness with your colleagues for appropriate
boundaries. *Conflict-of-interest* is a situation in which a person is
involved in multiple interests, financial or otherwise, and serving
one interest could involve working against another.

Past, Present, and Future

Almost everyone has had one or more jobs that they did not like, or in
which they had negative experiences. A worker should be free to
move from one job to the next, without the past interfering in
present and future jobs. Therefore, one must be cautious about

seeking references from a past colleague that the candidate declines, and from taking information from external sources on the candidate's abilities or reputation. Workers have the liberty to seek better workplaces without threat of repercussion.

Moral Relativism

Moral relativism is the difference between true and false; right and wrong. Then Cardinal Ratzinger decried the onset of what he termed the "dictatorship of relativism." Moral relativism can be difficult to identify, but usual involves action that is self-serving and without regard for the truth and common good. An honest and upright person, will maintain the truthful and right action in all cases.

Work Without Pay or Over-Working

The (FLSA) Fair Labor Standards Act of 1938, 29 U.S.C. § 203, is a United States labor law that creates the right to a minimum wage, and time-and-a-half overtime pay when working over forty hours in a week. This act prohibited most employment of minors, terming it oppressive child labor. Within the fair labor standards, breaks are allowable at certain intervals of work, and meal break is mandatory after every so many hours of continuous work. The Department of Labor is a good source of information on wage and hour standards. Policies and laws can be searched at *govinfo.gov*.

Power Struggles

Power struggles are not therapeutically-minded. You are allowed to know more than your superiors, but you should be gentle and reserved when communicating your knowledge. Conversations should be a give-and-take pleasant exchange of concern or information. Be aware that if you take a job beneath your level of education or experience, that there may be power struggles. You should avoid power struggles, as well as co-dependence, sycophant behavior, control, blaming or reversing blame, narcissism, manipulation, blackmailing, interrogation, retaliation, corruption, lying, terrorizing, bullying, identity confusion, factitious/feigning ideas, discrediting, undermining, gossiping, extortion, and so on. *Extortion:* the act of obtaining something by means of force or threat. Choose your battles carefully, and be comfortable in who you are; permitting the same in others. Employees should keep personal detailed notes of anything odd towards them at work.

Seriousness of Evaluations

The gravest mistake that a supervisor, manager, or employer can make is an incorrect evaluation. Evaluations should be honest and accurate interpretations of the employees work performance and character. *Nota bene* - a Latin phrase meaning 'note well.'

An employer may not be concerned about staff person # ___ 's work file, but to that employee, it could mean their future income and life success. Evaluations and staff files are serious matters.

Time Frame
Get to know your individual staff's education and work history. This will give you a good frame of reference about what they know and where they have been.

Next, consider how long this staff person has been with your company, and what is a reasonable amount of time to set performance expectations.

Then, if you say that will grade an employee on a certain set timeframe, for example, from March through April work; please make certain that you are only grading work from March through April. If the employee performed well during the timeframe that you pre-determined, then great! If they did not perform well during that timeframe, was it an outlier, where they normally perform better?

Character and Behavior

If you take the leap into judging and documenting on an employee's character or behavior, there should be real and specific data that you site.

If you site information that is hearsay, evasive, or antagonistic, no good will come from this. Likewise, if you site behavior that is due to a disability, then you open yourself up for lawsuit. Suggesting behavior or ways of acting, is inappropriate, unless it is to teach a commonly used interpersonal skill.

If you site character or behavior that is not specific and real, then you are just abusing and/or harassing your staff.

Bad Strategy

Evaluating a staff person by method of 'strategy' is both unethical and a waste of time. Deceit, trickery, degradation, misattributing, yelling, inconsistency, intimidation, and confusion, are all bad evaluation strategies.

Transparency in the workplace can be seen as honest and helpful communication between supervisors and employees. The website *Entrepreneur.com* defines the five characteristics of a transparent workplace as: communication, honesty, regular feedback, respect and admitting wrongs. Oftentimes, employers will fight to the end for the last word. But, admitting wrongs is the sign of effective and moral leadership.

When the leaders in a workplace act in a transparent manner, the workplace and its employees benefit. The result is faster problem solving, better teamwork, healthy working relationships, trust, and improved performance. A 2012 article on *Forbes.com* discusses workplace transparency, stating, "trust and transparency have become popular workplace demands as employees seek to be aware of what is real and true." If you spend each day at a job full of dishonest people, double standards, and a lack of communication; you have failed in trust and transparency. A transparent workplace leads to happier employees, right action, and increased production.

Feedback should be related to the issue(s) at hand, and not a catastrophic statement of the employee's 'uselessness' or other negative and mean generalizations.

Evaluative Standards

You will hear time and again, that evaluations should be in review of professional standards of ethics and practice, and the company standards. If a profession has a national association, there are likely to be written Standards of Practice, and a Code of Ethics, with which you can use as a guide.

Company standards should be in alignment with legal, lawful, just actions, and in the values which you model yourselves. Businesses exist to provide services and goods for a better world. Thus, every company's standards should be a descriptor of such a mission.

Incidents

If an incident has occurred in the workplace, get the names of all involved employees. Interview each of them alone, asking them, not interrogating them, about what has happened. How can you identify who is lying or withholding information?

Look at the employee with sincere interest in what they are saying, and with genuine concern for them. There will be a sense of honesty in your perception of objective and truthful answers.

If an employee says that they are in danger, it is important that you believe them. It is always better to air on the side of safety. But remain confidential to protect all those involved.

Developing Communications Skills

Communication is not only important among co-workers, but it is a key to teaching skills between supervisors and their employees. According to *toolshero.com*, the 7 C's of communication include:
1. Completeness
2. Concreteness
3. Courtesy
4. Correctness
5. Clarity
6. Consideration
7. Conciseness

Consider training programs in good management communication. Remember that evaluations are to ensure achievement of key goals, and to provide guidance and training to the employee.

Debriefing

Debriefing is a post-critical-incident support group. Debriefing is led by two to three speakers who are trained in emergency counseling, and is usually carried out within three to seven days of a critical incident. Debriefing is not counselling, but is a supportive presentation of what has happened, after workers have had enough time to take in the experience. Debriefing is a structured, voluntary discussion aimed at putting an abnormal event into an organized presentation, to help with emotional support.

The leaders of a debriefing may explain:

- o What has happened
- o Who was involved
- o Outcome and data if available
- o What have we learned?
- o What can we do?
- o What if? ......
- o What to expect
- o Referrals needed

Navigating Difficult Conversations

According to *Conflict Tango*, 85% of professionals worldwide stated that they experience conflict at work firsthand. Many of us find ourselves in situations at the workplace where we believe someone has wronged us or treated us badly. Experts advise you
to get the courage to have an honest conversation, when you are ready to discuss the offense. If you do not discuss it, the offending person may never know that they have upset you.

GetSmarter.com says to consider these 5 things before having a conversation:
1. Wait and let go of your emotions
2. Prepare what you want to say
3. Open your mind
4. Monitor your body language
5. Think about how you feel/felt

J. Rossi of Carnegie Mellon University, says that in preparation
for a conversation, you should examine your assumptions, emotions, prejudice, bias and barriers to understanding the person you want to confront. It is important to be aware of any competition you feel towards another, as the basis of bias in your upset. Ms. Rossi states that there are four options in communication, but the best result is one of assertiveness.

Aggressive: I win/you lose; hurts others
Assertive: I win/you win; balanced, fair, open and honest
Passive: I lose/you lose; hurts self-esteem
Passive/Aggressive: I lose/you lose; hurts everyone

Riley & Lee, Ombuds at Berkley University of California, say that there are benefits to having difficult conversations, such as: enhanced trust, empathy, collaboration, understanding, and positive change. An *Ombud* ("*ombudsman*" or "*ombudsperson*") is a designated neutral or impartial mediator. When you speak with someone, be cautious of your intention vs. the possible impact. Your intentions may be more for your benefit than another's. Your words can have a negative impact on the person with whom you will confront.

Importance of Humility in Workplace

In a *Harvard Business Review* article, (EQ) Emotional Intelligence guru Daniel Goleman, answers the question, 'What makes a good leader?' Goleman identifies self-awareness as the preeminent leadership skill and says, "People with a high degree of self-awareness know their weaknesses and aren't afraid to talk about them." Humility helps us to set aside your personal feelings, and look at yourself objectively.

Pope Francis, in a TED talk recorded in 2017, said that humility is not a weakness; rather, it is a kind of fortitude. He said, "Please, allow me to say it loud and clear: the more powerful you are, the more your actions will have an impact on people, the more responsible you are to act humbly. If you don't, your power will ruin you, and you will ruin the other."

Helio F. Garcia, Executive Director of *Logos Institute for Crisis Management and Executive Leadership*, says, "The best leaders have a temperament that blends both power and humility that allows them to create a culture of accountability in all directions." Helio says that "the best leaders exhibit humility; the best-handled crises are those where humility prevails."

In 1999, the *Institute of Medicine* published '*To Err Is Human*' report where the authors alleged that several thousand Americans die each year because of hospital errors, and that one of the leading errors was the spread of bacterial infections. A doctor from Cedars-Sinai Medical Center theorized two psychological reasons for this suspected error: 1) healthcare professionals think they wash their hands more than they actually do, and 2) they lack the humility to accept that they are the cause for the spread of infection. This example of humility illustrates how important regulation of our ego and humility can be.

Humility has been praised again and again as the real core of success in the business world. Successful leaders set aside their ego and direct their attention to the more important matters in truth and right action.

David Packard, an electrical engineer, and founder of Hewlett-Packard, was quoted to say that you should not gloat about anything you have done, but instead go on to do more great things.

A humble person is securely settled in a primary relationship with God. After all, God is the center of life and being, and should be given credit for all the good things in which we partake. Humility is the foundation on which all other virtues develop, and upon which we learn to accurately interpret others and understand our own needs.

Humility is realizing that we need God, and that we belong to Him.

Generosity accompanies all humility. Adam Grant, a Wharton professor, and a popular social science writer, says, "Generosity is earned, not claimed. Leave it to other people to describe you as a giver—that's the highest form of praise." Therefore, I implore to all of you: allow others to proclaim your greatness.

In a 2009 *Harvard Business Review* article by Dame and Gedmin, there is suggested six basic principles in humility:

1. Know what you don't know
2. Resist falling for your own publicity
3. Never underestimate the competition
4. Embrace and promote a spirit of service
5. Listen to all ideas
6. Be passionately eager to learn more

Take and apply these suggestions, not in a spirit of cleverness or shame, but in the spirit of perpetual growth in humility. We must acknowledge our littleness in a planet of billions of needy people. Needy for help that you may be able to provide, or perhaps, needy for the little things which we take for granted.

Be grateful for what you have; so many have less and are suffering greatly.

Stress Management

The *American Institute for Stress*, says that stress can be physical, mental, and emotional strain or tension. There are four types of stress: Acute Stress: fight or flight, sudden and intense stress; Chronic Stress: daily life stress which will even effect your health; Eustress: good stress such as a new job or relationship; and Distress: bad stress such as work and financial problems, divorce and injury.

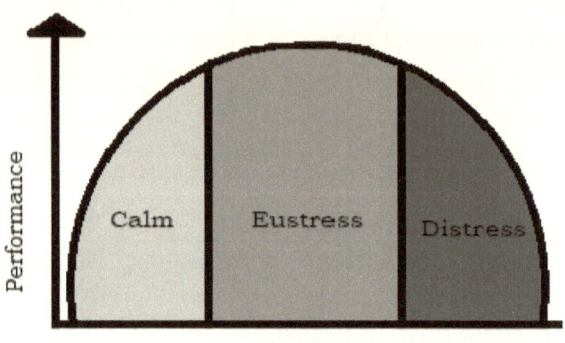

Figure b.) Shows performance increases when good stress increases.

What can you do to help stress and prevent burnout?

- ❖ Sleep a minimum of 7-8 hours per night
- ❖ Eat a diet of lean protein, colorful vegetables and fruits, good fats, calcium, nuts and seeds, beans, whole grains
- ❖ Avoid caffeine, nicotine, sugar, alcohol, drugs
- ❖ Exercise regularly, cardio and strength exercises
- ❖ Have quiet time, deep breaths, meditation, journaling
- ❖ Participate in fun activities that you enjoy
- ❖ Soak in a warm shower or bath
- ❖ Relax with aroma therapeutic scents
- ❖ Stay current on the news events around the world
- ❖ Go for a walk, listen to music, or see a favorite show
- ❖ Visit your family and friends frequently
- ❖ Talk with a counselor
- ❖ Maintain regular visits with your physician
- ❖ Go to church every Sunday
- ❖ Organize your closet and home, keep it neat and clean
- ❖ Volunteer and get involved

Resources

TIP # 14

Be the best you that you can be.
You are the only baseline for judgement,
and you are the sole determinant
of who you are meant to be.

Americans with Disabilities Act

The Americans with Disabilities Act (ADA) became law in 1990. The ADA is a civil rights law that prohibits discrimination against individuals with disabilities in all areas of public life, including jobs, schools, transportation, and all public and private places that are open to the general public. The purpose of the law is to make sure that people with disabilities have the same rights and opportunities as everyone else. The ADA is to give civil rights protections to individuals with disabilities, similar to those provided to individuals on the basis of race, sex, national origin, age, and religion. It guarantees equal opportunity for individuals with disabilities in public accommodations, employment, transportation, state and local government services, and telecommunications *(ADA National Network)*. Title I of the ADA law is regarding accommodations in employment settings. (JAN) *askjan.org* - Job Accommodation Network is a service of West Virginia University, and may be helpful for ADA information.

All disabilities are to be treated with the same regard. This is to includes both accommodations for a physical disability and mental disability. Request your accommodations as soon as you know that you will need them. Speak with your employer about your needs at the most appropriate time. Remember to highlight your assets, and what you bring to the job as well.

Ticket to Work

Ticket to Work is a program of the Social Security Administration. Anyone age 18 through 64 who receives Social Security Disability Insurance (SSDI) and/or Supplemental Security Income (SSI), because of a disability, is eligible to participate in the Ticket to Work program. Participation in the Ticket to Work program is free and voluntary. Ticket to Work Help Line at 866-968-7842 or 866-833-2967 (TTY), to verify your eligibility.

Ticket to Work connects you with employment services to help you decide if working is right for you, to prepare you for work, and to find a job or maintain success while you are working.

You can receive services such as career counseling, vocational rehabilitation, job placement and training from authorized Ticket to Work service providers, such as Employment Networks (EN) or your state Vocational Rehabilitation (OVR) agency.

Office of Vocational Rehabilitation

Office of Vocational Rehabilitation, or OVR, provides vocational rehabilitation services to help persons with disabilities prepare for, obtain, and maintain employment. It is a federal program that provides leadership and resources to state and other agencies to deliver these services.

The OVR assists customers in selecting their choice of vocational goals, services and service providers. An Individualized Plan for Employment (IPE) is developed, outlining a vocational objective, service plan, providers and customer responsibilities. Certain services are subject to a Financial Needs Test (FNT). Funding is available to people in certain areas, and may include financial assistance with training, equipment, license fees, and transportation.

Services through OVR may include counseling and guidance, diagnostic services, assessments, information and referral, job development and placement, and personal services, such as readers or sign language interpreters, are usually provided at no cost to the OVR customer. Below are areas in which OVR may assist:

- Diagnostic Testing - Medical, psychological, audiological, neurological may be options, respective to your condition and state office.
- Vocational Evaluation - Aptitude, career interests, academic exams, and work tolerance are the focus of a vocational evaluation.
- Counseling - Vocational counseling will help you to understand your abilities and potential, and develop good work habits.
- Restorative Service - This may include physical and occupational therapy, drug and alcohol treatment, wheelchairs, and more.

- Training - Academic, college, technical, on-the-job, and independent living skills.
- Placement Assistance - Job-seeking programs, job clubs, interview and résumé counseling, tips for work applications.

(EEOC) Equal Employment Opportunity Commission

The United States Equal Employment Opportunity Commission is a federal agency that administers and enforces civil rights laws against workplace discrimination. *EEOC.gov*

EEOC handles discrimination complaints for such areas as race/ethnicity, age, and disability. Complaints are investigated and determined appropriate for filing. EEOC then takes action for resolving such a charge. If you have an (ADA) Americans with Disabilities Act complaint, it will likely be filed with the EEOC. ADA laws and regulations can be found online at *ADA.gov*, a United States Department of Justice Civil Rights Division.

EEOC can assist small businesses with tips on employment requirements, and EEOC maintains employment facts and figures that may be helpful to know.

The federal component of the EEOC provides outreach and training, and oversees the operations and laws.

Tax Incentives

Work Opportunity Tax Credit (WOTC) is a Federal tax credit available to employers, as incentive to hire individuals from certain targeted groups, who have consistently faced significant barriers to employment. Form 8850 available at *IRS.gov* is a pre-screening and certification request for WOTC. Tax incentives offered do change over time, so review current IRS precedents.

Earning Your Degree

(GED) General Education Development - General Education Development tests are commonly considered equal to a high school diploma. If you did not graduate from high school, then you should find your most local GED testing center. Most counties in each state have GED classes, practice tests, and testing facilities. There is a small fee for GED classes and testing, depending on where you reside.

Vocational Education - Vocational education is training that prepares you to work in skilled labor jobs, such as mechanics, esthetics, culinary, and machinery. Vocational education is usually pursued in cooperation with your high school classes. However, there are technical training centers for education beyond high school. Vocational education coordinators can assist in job placement.

College - Colleges may offer 4-year programs leading to a Bachelor's degree, or a 2-year program leading to an Associate's degree. Many colleges also offer graduate degree programs. *Liberal Arts* refers to schools which provide a broad range of elective courses, in preparation for a well-rounded knowledge base.

University - A University acquires such designation when it has accredited schools within its college. Examples of different schools may be: a school of education, school of business, or school of medicine. A university may offer any level of degrees.

Public - Public colleges are funded by local and state governments, and usually offer lower cost tuition, especially for students who are local to the state.

Private - Private colleges rely on tuition, fees, and private sources of funding. Private colleges are often, but not always, of religious affiliation. Other private colleges may be ranked by academic merit admissions, such as the well-known 'ivy leagues'.

Community College - A community college is associated with the county in which you reside. Community colleges offer classes to the public for lifelong learning, but also offer college-credit classes. Community college may be a good option for students with financial constraints, or for those who wish to remain close to home while studying.

Education Loans

There are two types of student loans: federal loans sponsored by the federal government, and private student loans. Student loans may be offered as part of a total financial aid package that may include grants, scholarships, and/or work study opportunities.

Federal loans can be subsidized or unsubsidized; interest does not accrue on subsidized loans while the students are in school. Federal student loan interest is generally not deductible; interest rates are established by Congress and listed in § 20 U.S.C. § 1087E (b). The amount a student can borrow depends on their educational level, visit *studentloans.gov*. Payback for the student loans can be transferred to a third party company, with easy-to-manage interest rates. Loans can be deferred during times of job loss, or for other dedicated reasons, but this is only for a limited amount of time. Student loans must be repaid as agreed upon in your loan contract.

Private student loans and scholarships may be respective to your school. Applying students may also find an abundance of public scholarships in their school student services offices; these scholarships will require an application process. Brand businesses like Pepsi Co., foundations, charities, and endowment funds, also offer applications for scholarships. The more popular a scholarship, the less chance of your being awarded it. The internet makes possible the ease of broad searching; so do your scholarship research thoroughly. Browse the reviews on private student lenders, or speak with your local bank for information on loans.

Tips for quick learning and memorizing:
- Focus diligently on your studies
- Develop acronyms for phrases
- Relate what you already know to the new
- Teach others what you are trying to learn
- Use pictures rather than words
- Rhyme phrases that you need to remember
- Write things down
- Do not stress

Veterans

By law, veterans who are disabled or who served in active duty in the Armed Forces, or in military campaigns, are entitled to preference over non-veterans both in hiring from competitive job lists, and in retention during reductions in workforce (*military.com*). (VOW)Veteran Opportunity to Work, to Hire Heroes Act of 2011, entitles them to preference over others in hiring for many state and federal government jobs.

(TBI) Traumatic Brain Injury

Traumatic Brain Injury affects more than 1 million people per year. The severity of brain injury is graded on a spectrum from mild to severe. Brain injury can result from physical impact to the brain as a result of falls, motor vehicle accidents, sports, attack/assault, and organic decline in dementias. Other less explored causes of brain injury result from PTSD, soldiers at war, and prolonged mental distress or disease.

TBI may appear as amnesia, inability to speak or understand language, mental confusion, difficulty thinking and understanding, inability to create new memories, abnormal laughing and crying, aggression, impulsivity, irritability, lack of restraint, repetition of words or actions, fatigue, difficulty concentrating or completing tasks, a decline in cognitive abilities from previous ability, anger, anxiety, apathy, and loneliness.

If you have sustained a brain injury, or experience PTSD or any other emotional illness, you should contact a physician or qualified treatment provider as soon as possible. Trauma effects our brain structure, neural pathways, brain waves, immune system, toxin elimination, cells and nervous system.

Recovery, or some amount of recovery, is possible for many people, while others remain limited. It is important to become educated on brain injury for yourself and your family and support system.

Because symptoms of brain injury may remain with you for many years, it is important to be aware of your limitations in the workplace. Your setbacks and weakness could be related to this injury.

Recommendations for treatment, depending on where you are in the recovery process, may include:

- Neurorehabilitation
- Physical and Occupational Therapy
- Psychiatry and/or Neurology
- Mental Health Counseling
- Safety Alert devices
- Safety Planning
- Ongoing monitoring and screening
- Stress Management
- Disability interventions
- Nutrition and Holistic care
- Compassionate and supportive friends
- Good daily activities

Career Testing

Career interest and aptitude testing is available in some locations, and even on internet sites. Watch your local newspapers or school bulletins for advertisements on career testing.

You may find career testing centers at any or more of the following locations: career services offices at universities, colleges, community college, and libraries; as well in some psychological testing centers. These services are often advertised in newspapers and newsletters.

The Princeton Review offers many good services for students. Their website includes personal and innovative services, such as: tutor-finder, test prep, and admission products and services to help students achieve their academic goals. On *princetonreview.com*, there is a short quiz to assess your 'Usual Style' of interests and personality, in order to assist in guiding you toward a particular career field.

Other websites that are frequented for career testing, include: Truity, MAPP Assessment, CareerFitter, 123Test, Sokanu, and Monster Jobs.

Whether a career test is in-person or online, there is nothing to fear. This is to be a relaxed test to assist you in the future with finding a most suitable career path for your well-being and success.

Just Say No

Drugs, alcohol, and nicotine are all substances that damage your body and mind. Caffeine also causes many bad symptoms and effects your functioning. Just say no to these substances. *samhsa.gov*

Finding a Specialist

Many health insurance companies offer a *Provider Referral Network* of doctors, and local hospitals provide a list of affiliated doctors and specialists. There are also many health websites on which mental health providers post their advertisements.
Questions to consider when seeking a provider:
Have friends and neighbors used them? Do they really listen to you and respond appropriately to your questions? Do they spend enough time with your family? Do they show respect? Do they ask about your treatment preferences and values?

FMLA

The Family and Medical Leave Act of 1993 is a United States labor law requiring covered employers to provide employees with job-protected and unpaid leave for qualified medical and family reasons. *dol.gov*

Planning for the Future

Tip # 15

Keep an accurate ledger of your banking transactions. Speak with a financial specialist to learn about money management and savings options.

Banking

Banks are plentiful, and may draw your business by location or ease of use, by family affiliation, or by good-market promotions.

Banking Regulators

The Office of the Comptroller of the Currency (OCC), the Federal Deposit Insurance Corporation (FDIC), and the banking departments of various states regulate financial institutions. Learn about consumer protection at *federalreserveeducation.org*.

Checking Account

Checking Accounts are good for everyday transactions such as check-paid purchases, bill payments, and ATM withdrawals. Checking accounts come with a debit card, which can be used like a credit card, but money is subtracted from what you already have in your account, from your work-earnings and deposits. Checks can be ordered from your bank for a fee, or you can use an independent check company, and have your account number printed on the checks. Some checking accounts charge a monthly fee to keep open, especially if the $ amount in your account is low. *Direct deposit* of your work earnings can be arranged for direct entry into your personal bank account each payday.

Savings Account

A savings account is a deposit account held at a bank or other financial institution, and provides a minor profit interest gain. There may be a minimum amount of deposit required to open a savings account. Your financial institution may limit the number of withdrawals you can make from a savings account. In most cases, banks do not provide checks or debit cards with a savings account.

(CD) Certificate of Deposit

CDs can be opened with a banking institution and with some credit card companies. CDs are created upon your deposit of an amount of money, and are a timed savings account, with earned APY interest. You can choose a term length for your CD that is completely customized to your investment desires. There is usually a minimum amount of money, and on up, required to open a CD. *APY: Annual Percentage Yield.*

Credit Cards

Credit cards can be easy to open, and are convenient to have for everyday purchases. However, there are major risks associated with credit cards. Some risks include a high interest rate in addition to your purchase price, and in spending more money than you have to spend. It is wise that you get in the habit of using cash or a debit card for everyday purchases, so you do not spend more than you are able to pay back.

Care Credit

Care Credit © is a credit card for medical expenses. Care Credit is approved at each distinct medical purchase, for the agreed upon price, and timeframe of no-interest payments. Care Credit can be used for eye glasses, cosmetic and dental procedures, at prescription/drug retail stores, and more. The benefit of Care Credit vs. another credit card, is that interest charges can be deferred for a set amount of months. But, if you have not paid off your purchase within the set amount of months of no-interest, then interest will be thus applied, and at a very high rate.

Pay Pal

Pay Pal © is another form of lending for online purchases. Pay Pal can be used for both purchases, and for small business earnings of online stores. You must register for Pay Pal online at *paypal.com*. Purchases on Pay Pal can be deferred in payment, with a specific promotional offering at the time of use.

Insurance

Marketplace Insurance Plans

Healthcare.gov Marketplace Insurance Coverage is a health insurance exchange website operated under the United States federal government, under the provisions of the Patient Protection and Affordable Care Act, which currently serves the residents of the U.S. Plan options vary according to region and cooperating insurance companies. Premium financing is based on your level of income. Deductibles are often high, but the plans are comparable to every good plan available to the public. Premium tax credits can be applied to the monthly premium charges, further assisting with monthly insurance costs. The Marketplace is a great option for anyone seeking good health insurance, and who may not have an insurance options available from their employer.

Health Sharing Insurance Plans

Health Sharing insurance plans are new and non-traditional, and usually Christian affiliated. In some cases, health sharing insurances may be more restrictive with the benefits offered, but are significantly less costly; and contribute to a greater good, both economically and spiritually. Health sharing insurances are now covering with more than 1,000,000 people and counting. Health Sharing is voluntary among members for *eligible* medical expenses. Specifically, members send in monthly 'shares' or premiums which are distributed to, or on behalf of other members, with medical expenses and in need of benefit payments.

These models are built upon the principle of people with similar beliefs and values coming together to share in each other's burdens. This concept projects more responsibility and accountability onto providers to perform the best care. Families can become members in health sharing plans for approximately $300-500 per month. Popular plans include Christ Medicus *cmfcuro.com*, Samaritan Ministries s*amaritanministries.org*, and Trinity HealthShare *trinityhealthshare.org*

Communitas Primary Care

Individuals and businesses can apply to use this newer model of (DPC) Direct Primary Care. DPC can be used by itself or paired with another insurance plan. By using both, people have coverage for severe accidents, and quality medical care for general illness. DPC allows you to talk to your doctor at any time, have home visits, and to reach out for advice for any illness. Businesses use DPC to better ensure the health of their employees and provide them with an inexpensive but quality healthcare. Insurance models that can be paired with DPC include: Health Sharing, Short Term Medical, and Employer/Self-Insurance. Communitas can provide services for 90 percent of your medical needs. For the emergency needs they cannot help with however, they will negotiate better rates for you from your preferred specialist.

communitasprimarycare.com

Non-Health Insurance

Professional Liability
Professional liability insurance, or professional indemnity insurance, is a form of liability insurance which helps protect professional service-providing individuals and companies from bearing the full cost of defending against a negligence claim made by a client. Professional liability does not protect you in a criminal proceeding though. Professional liability insurance is categorized and offered by type of profession and according to policy outlines. Policy finances are set by your choice of yearly fee along with the paired range of legal coverage. Not all lawsuit finances may be covered by your insurance plan; verify this ahead of time.

Auto, Renters, Home Owners Insurance
Auto insurance is mandatory in many states. Points given for traffic violations and vehicle accidents may negatively reflect on the cost of your auto insurance. *Home Owners Insurance* is mandatory in many regions, especially if you use a mortgage lender. Home owner's coverage may protect your dwelling, personal items, family liability, and in some cases guest medical coverage. *Renters* insurance covers financial limits of your choice based on your asset value. Renter's insurance however, only covers your personal items inside the dwelling. *Lemonade.com* offers home and renter's insurance to urban dwellers, and is rated A-Exceptional and a (PBC) Public Benefit Corporation. Consider all of your options for insurance coverage.

Fire and Flood Insurance
Flood insurance is often a separate purchase insurance, and is usually not retroactive following a flood incident. The average cost of a flood insurance policy is $700 per year, but this can be misleading. If you are in a low-risk area and need minimal coverage levels, your cost will most likely be much less. The opposite is true if your property is a high-risk zone and has a higher value. Fire and Flood insurance may be covered jointly in certain regions, especially those where wildfires occur.

FEMA

FEMA Federal Emergency Management Agency is a department within the U.S. Department of Homeland Security, and provides disaster assistance services.*disasterassistance.gov*

Life Insurance

Term Life Insurance may be purchased for an initial low premium, and covers such things as home mortgage, auto loan, educational credit, and outstanding debt; but only for a certain amount of time. *Permanent Life Insurance* offers stable premium rates, and covers you and your loved ones for the life of the policy. Permanent Life Insurance may cover a loved one's financial needs, funeral expenses, estate planning, contributions to charity, and access to accumulated cash value. The details of these and all insurance policies are more finely detailed according with your chosen insurance provider.

Critical Illness Insurance

Critical Illness Insurance can pay for costs not covered by traditional insurance. The money can also be used for non-medical costs related to the illness, including transportation, child care, and out-of-town housing. If you purchase this insurance through an employer, you may only be able to use it while employed. But on the upside, your plan may allow for coverage of multiple illnesses, over the course of your life, up to a certain financial amount.

Short and Long Term Disability

Short and long-term disability coverage, is offered while you are employed, and perhaps only when employed in a permanent full-time capacity. Enrollment in these coverage plans is usually a low monthly cost, but payout of the coverage, if disabled, is based on percentages of what you earn while working, and is time-limited.

Travel Insurance

Travel insurance may cover lost luggage, cancelled flights, travel medical costs, and trip cancellation coverage. Some professional associations also offer travel insurance and auto rental; inquire with your unique professional association.

Speak with a certified insurance agent or representative for more insurance information on all of these and more programs.

Retirement

Pension
Pension is an older type of retirement plan, usually offered to public sector employees. With a pension plan, the employer contributes money to the pension while you are working. Your pension withholding is usually a choice percentage of your wages. Your *pension* will be paid to you monthly after retirement. Pension payout amount is calculated based on: 1) years of service with the company, 2) your age, and 3) your working salary. Generally, the later in life that you retire, the greater the amount your pension pay will be. Being *vested* in your pension plan, usually assumes that you have been with your employer for at least 5 years, and any contributions to the plan are 100% yours. Taxes are paid on pension funds when paid-out at retirement.

401(k)
A traditional 401(k) retirement plan defers income tax until retirement pay-out as well. Some employers will match an employee's contribution into their 401(k) accounts. Percentage of wage withholding into this retirement plan usually starts at a low initial percentage, and may be increased annually up to a capped percentage contribution. The U.S. Securities and Exchange Commission sets the rules and regulates of 401(k) programs. *investor.gov*

Deferred Compensation
Deferred compensation is an additional retirement withholding, from your wages, into a savings plan. The amount of withholding is your choice, for example, $100 per paycheck. Depending on who manages your deferred compensation program, there may be options to invest a small portion of your withholdings into stocks and funds. This money is subject to market fluctuations though. Depending on current trends, your account managers may have stable or fixed accounts in which you <u>do not</u> have to invest in stocks, thus not taking the risk of losing money. Under only certain circumstances, outlined in your plan, can you withdraw your funds early, and possibly then pay a penalty withdrawal fee.

403(b)

A 403(b) plan is another type of pre-tax retirement plan, often used by non-profit companies. This retirement plan requires less administrative costs to operate than a 401(k) plan.

Roth IRA

A Roth IRA is a deferred compensation program in which your deferred compensation is *after-tax* money, and will not be subject to taxing when paid-out at retirement.

Flexible Spending

Your employer or local credit unions, may offer accounts termed *flexible spending*, in which you contribute a portion of your earnings into an account marked only for the use which you are saving. For example, you may want to save for your children's education, for orthodontics, or for holiday or travel finances.

Mutual Funds

Investors buy shares in mutual funds. Each share represents an investor's partial ownership in the fund and in the income which it generates. The combined holdings of the mutual fund are known as its portfolio. A mutual fund is a company that gathers money from many investors and invests the money in securities such as stocks and bonds. Learn how to avoid fraud at *investors.gov*. There are faith-based mutual fund companies, so that you can invest and support only in those which share in your moral standards. Some examples of the faith-based mutual fund companies include: Ave Maria Mutual Funds (symbol AVEDX) *avemariafunds.com*, and Aquinas Value (AQEIX), which follow the guidelines of the U.S. Conference of Catholic Bishops.

Speak with a knowledgeable financial advisor for more information.

Small Business Administration

The U.S. Small Business Administration (SBA) supports America's small business startups. The SBA can connect entrepreneurs with lenders and funding. *sba.gov* Or, learn about programs, contracting services, marketing plans, business counseling, and take classes at the SBA. Other resources include Women's Business Center, Veteran Business Outreach, and Small Business Development.

Legal Aid

Local county legal boards supply a listing of volunteer or *pro-bono* lawyers, who will speak with you and possibly provide services to those who do not have the finances to hire a lawyer. Some law firms will take payment on a *contingency fee* basis, meaning only if they/you win.

Tools of the Job

TIP # 16

Begin preparing for your job interview a few days beforehand. Collate your documents, press your suit, visualize answering the questions, and practice stress management techniques.

(IRT) Interview Readiness Tool ©

Complete	✓
Cover Letter	
Résumé or CV	
Thought about interview answers	
Bought a nice suit	
Cleaned and pressed suit	
Reference #1	
Reference #2	
Reference #3	
Back-up Reference	
Prepared your references	
Learned about the employer	
Related employer mission to yourself	
Understand the job description	
Sent a Thank You note after the interview	

(JRT) Job Readiness Tool ©

Understand	✔
I have read this book.	
Types of References	
How to Get a Good Recommendation	
Marketing & Professionalism	
How to Interview	
Role of Employer	
Role of Human Resources	
Self-Development and a Good Character	
Labor Markets and finding Meaning in Life	
Banking, Finances, Healthcare, Insurances	
Education, Schools, Helpful Resources	
Say NO to Drugs, Alcohol, Nicotine	

Afterword

I personally know how difficult it is to work in this current day. I am a professional with a disability. However, I do not think my disability has been as much a challenge as has been my time with difficult coworkers. I want to tell you, that if you face challenges at work; you are not alone. You are not alone.

Pope Francis' visit to Panama for World Youth Day XXXIV was marked by these words: "*the enrichment of intergenerational dialogue, the enrichment of exchange and the value of realizing that we need one another, that we have to work to create channels and spaces that encourage dreaming of and working for tomorrow, starting today. And this, not in isolation, but rather side by side, creating a common space. A space that is not simply taken for granted, or won in a lottery, but a space for which you too must fight...promote a social contract in which everyone has the chance to dream of a tomorrow. Another world is possible...The right to a future is also a human right.*" The Pope urged young people to take part in building a better world. He said, "*These horizons can enrich the path ahead through a respectful and compassionate gaze upon others.*

Pray and act so that your lives glorify God, in the good work that you do, and the love that you show towards one another.

My parents are my role models. My mom and dad both put themselves through college and graduate school, while working full-time. My dad was a Staff Sergeant in the Air Force Reserves, and my mom gave life to three children. They built our house, and had a warm, healthy meal on the table every single night. Our family attended church every Sunday, and frequently during the week as well. My parents were kind, generous, hard-working people. They watched their budget, and made every sacrifice, putting themselves last. My parents are role models for all young adults today who are seeking a good future through hard-work and dedication.

I encourage everyone to get educated and earn a degree(s). No one can take away the dignity of your earned degree! If you earn a college degree, it will always be yours to carry with pride... for the remainder of your life.

If you face challenges with employment, finances, work references, or in any facet of your life, DO NOT lose hope. God put you on the planet for a purpose, but you must do His will to the best of your ability. Always continue on your journey; you must find the life you were meant to live. When you get your good recommendation; do great work and prove your reference true. Hold your head high always, and work for the common good of all with integrity and skill.

The *common good* in philosophy, economics, and political science, refers to what is shared and beneficial for all, for most members of a given community. There is no elimination of certain people in the common good community. Rather, in a society for the common good, there is a place for everyone, and everyone benefits.

In *The Common Good* (2018), author Robert Reich makes a case for the expansion of America's 'moral imagination.' He demonstrates that the common good constitutes the "very essence of any society." Societies, he says, "undergo virtuous cycles that reinforce the common good, as well as vicious cycles that undermine it." In a society or community that works for the common good, no one is harmed, rejected, or abandoned.

The book entitled, *Together! Social Virtue and The Common Good* (2008), relays to leaders that the social message of the Gospel is a basis and motivation of action for the good. I urge all employers to take a second look at the social situations in your work environment, and what type of virtuous people and community you want to build. There is a just society possible for all people, where everyone is doing what our God wills, and making meaning in their life.

Additional Resources

The Academic Job Search Handbook: Fifth Edition; Vick, Furlong, Lurie (2016). University of Pennsylvania Press.

Body of Work: Finding the Thread that Ties Your Story Together, Pamela Slim (2013). Portfolio.

Bring Your Human to Work: 10 Surefire Ways to Design a Workplace that is Good for People, Great for Business, and Just Might Change the World, Erica Keswin (2018). McGraw-Hill Education.

The Bully at Work, 2nd Edition, Namie & Namie (2009). Source Books Inc.

The Bully-Free Workplace, Namie & Namie (2011). John Wiley & Sons, Inc.

The Confidence Code: The Science and Art of Self-Assurance-What Women Should Know, Katty Kay and Claire Shipman (2014). Harper Business.

Cracking the Academic Nut: A Guide to Preparing for your Academic Career, Margaret Newhouse (1997). Office of Career Services, Harvard University.

Crossing the Unknown Sea: Work as a Pilgrimage of Identity, David Whyte (2002). Riverhead Books.

Curriculum Vitae Handbook, Rebecca Anthony and Gerald Roe (1998). Rudi Publishing.

Daniel Amen MD Mental Wellness Clinics *amenclinics.com*

David & Goliath: Underdogs, Misfits and the Art of Battling Giants, Malcolm Gladwell (2015). Back Bay Books.

Debriefing: Collected Stories, Susan Sontag (2018). Picador.

Die Empty: Unleash Your Best Work Every Day, Todd Henry (2015). Portfolio.

Drive: The Surprising Truth about What Motivates Us, Daniel Pink (2011). Riverhead Books.

Emotional Intelligence: Why it Can Matter More Thank IQ (10th Anniversary Edition), Daniel Goleman (2005). Bantam Books.

The Enneagram Institute *enneagraminstitute.com*

Excellence Everyday: Make the Daily Choice-Inspire Your employees and Amaze Your Customers, Lior Arrusy (2008). Information Today Inc.

The Fifth Discipline: The Art & Practice of the Learning Organization, Peter Senge (2006). The Crown Publishing Group.

Give & Take: Why Helping Others Drives Our Success, Adam Grant (2014). Penguin Books.

Good to Great: Why Some Companies Make the Leap... and Others Don't, Jim Collins (2001). Harper Collins Publishers.

Humility Rules: Saint Benedict's Twelve-Step Guide to Genuine Self-Esteem, Austine Wetta (2017). Ignatius Press.

How to Prepare Your Curriculum Vitae, Acy Jackson and Katheen Geckeis (2003). The McGraw-Hill Companies.

Humilitas, John Dickson (2011). Zondervan.

Laborem Exercens (Through Work), Pope John Paul II (1981). Vatican.

Moral Principles in Voting *ewtn.com/vote*

Neural Correlates of Admiration and Compassion, Mary Helen Immordino-Yang, Andrea McColl, Hanna Damasio, and Antonio Damasio PNAS published ahead of print April 20, 2009.

I Beg to Differ: Navigating Difficult Conversations with Truth and Love, Tim Muehlhoff (2014). InterVarsity Press.

People Skills: How to Assert Yourself, Listen to Others, and Resolve Conflicts, Robert Bolton (1986). Touchstone.

Presence: Bringing Your Boldest Self to Your Biggest Challenges, Amy Cuddy (2015). Little, Brown & Company.

Publications Manual of the (APA) American Psychological Association

Refuse to Choose!: Use All of Your Interests, Passions and Hobbies to Create the Life and Career of Your Dreams, Barbara Sher (2007). Rodale Books.

Saint Paul the Apostle, Pope Benedict XVI (2009). Our Sunday Visitor.

Scaling Up Excellence: Getting to More without Settling for Less, Sutton & Rao (2014). Crown Business.

Seedbeds of Virtue, Glendon & Blankenhorn (1995). Madison Books.

The Steps of Humility and Pride, Saint Bernard of Clairvaux (1989). Cistercian Publications.

Value-Based Coaching, Marilyn Edelson (2010). NASW Press.

Virtuous Leaders, Richard Kilbur (2012). APA Publishers.

Where to Start and What to Ask: An Assessment Handbook (Revised), Susan Lukas (2012). Norton, W.W. & Company, Inc.

Working Identity: Unconventional Strategies for Reinventing Your Career, Herminia Ibarra (2004). Harvard Business Review Press.

The 7 Habits of Highly Effective People, Stephen Covey (2000). Running Press Book Publishers.

120 Jobs that Won't Chain You to Your Desk, The Princeton Review (2007).

Register to Vote

Usa.gov/register-to-vote

About the Author

 **Tiffany A. Riebel**, MSW EAP CCTP is a Social Worker and Therapist. She attended college at Gannon University, and graduate school at Case Western Reserve University and the University of Pittsburgh.

Ms. Riebel has earned numerous certificates, including in Employee Assistance Programs from the National Catholic School of Social Service at the Catholic University of America; and Higher Education Teaching with Harvard University. She was an affiliate member during the founding of the Institute of Coaching at HMS, and is a participant in the (ICCE) International Center for Clinical Excellence. Ms. Riebel is a certified Lean Six Sigma Black Belt.

"How to Be a Great Reference, and Get a Great Reference" is a succinct and comprehensive compilation of information. There are great tips for new employees as well as seasoned employers. ...the skills that you speak to are so often overlooked by many employers and many of today's young people when interviewing.
                                                    -Laura Brovich, LMSW

The encyclical, Laborem Exercens presents the prime theory for the "dignity of work" - "How to be a Great Reference and Get a Great Reference" - offers a prime practical step by step process and plan to gain work and keep it.   -Larry Mayes, MPP

For Veterans, this book is a goldmine...you'll have the tools and wisdom you need to transition out of the military and engage in the civilian sector with confidence and assurance.
                                                    -Dr. Nick Stevens, Psy.D.

In "How to Be a Great Reference, and Get a Great Reference", Ms. Riebel covers a great deal of ground. She has pulled together outstanding information that will allow the reader to be well prepared for requesting a reference, interviewing for a job, and performing that job ethically. She gives thoughtful feedback for those who are writing references for students and employees. In particular, there are helpful checklists and tips that will assist any applicant in professional success.
                                                    -Wendy Concepcion, LMFT

16 Tips for Success

TIP # 1 It is very important for an employee to be aware of their actions at all times. Think about consequences before you act.

TIP # 2 Be willing to help another at any time. Offer to help before being asked, and give frequent reminders that you are available to them.

TIP # 3 Refrain from diagnosing or sharing diagnosis in your recommendation of a candidate, and in any professional environment. Do not diagnose your colleagues; their personal life is not your business.

TIP # 4 Introduce yourself to someone new every day. Make your number of good acquaintances exceed the bad.

TIP # 5 Take a course in record keeping. Record keeping is valuable to know for yourself, and in every business task.

TIP # 6 Evaluations of employees should represent honest, accurate, and objective interpretation of the employees' adherence to the ethics and professional standards of practice in their field.

TIP # 7 Do not accept or solicit colleagues for negative information about one another. This opens the channels for interpersonal problems and maleficence.

TIP # 8 Anonymity is a more specific form of confidentiality, meaning completely anonymous. If you see your doctor out in public, they may show no knowledge of you for the sake of *anonymity* or confidentiality.

TIP # 9 Those who are shy or needing confidence, should perform *"as if"* they are confident, well-spoken professionals.

TIP # 10 Have several different people review your résumé. Each may have different and helpful feedback.

TIP # 11 Enhance your vocabulary by reading and writing. Always keep a dictionary and thesaurus on your desk for quick reference.

TIP # 12 Spend time reflecting on your day. Consider on a regular basis what you could do to improve yourself.

TIP # 13 Speak well of your customers and colleagues. They are your professional life and your personal success.

TIP # 14 Be the best you that you can be. You are the only baseline for judgement, and you are the sole determinant of who you are meant to be.

Tip # 15 Keep an accurate ledger of your banking transactions. Speak with a financial specialist to learn about money management and savings options.

TIP # 16 Begin preparing for your job interview a few days beforehand. Collate your documents, press your suit, visualize answering the questions, and practice stress management techniques.

www.ingramcontent.com/pod-product-compliance
Lightning Source LLC
Chambersburg PA
CBHW030756180526
45163CB00003B/1049